TRUMPETS
OVER THE SEA

BOOKS BY J. B. PRIESTLEY

FICTION

Adam in Moonshine
Benighted
The Good Companions
Angel Pavement
Faraway
Wonder Hero
Laburnum Grove
They Walk in the City
The Doomsday Men
Let the People Sing
Blackout in Gretley
Daylight on Saturday
Three Men in New Suits

Bright Day
Jenny Villiers
Festival at Farbridge
The Other Place: short stories
The Magicians
Low Notes on a High Level
Saturn Over the Water
The Thirty-First of June
The Shapes of Sleep
Sir Michael and Sir George
Lost Empires
It's an Old Country
Out of Town (The Image Men - I)

PLAYS

The Roundabout
Duet in Floodlight
Spring Tide
Mystery at Greenfingers
The Long Mirror
The Rose and Crown
The High Toby
Bright Shadow

Dragon's Mouth (with Jacquetta Hawkes)
Private Rooms
Treasure on Pelican
Try it Again
Mother's Day
A Glass of Bitter
Mr Kettle and Mrs Moon

COLLECTED PLAYS

Volume I	Volume II	Volume III
Dangerous Corner	Laburnum Grove	Cornelius
Eden End	Bees on the Boat Deck	People at Sea
Time and the Conways	When we are Married	They Came to a City
I Have Been Here Before	Good Night Children	Desert Highway
Johnson over Jordan	The Golden Fleece	An Inspector Calls
Music at Night	How are they at Home?	Home is Tomorrow
The Linden Tree	Ever Since Paradise	Summer Day's Dream

ESSAYS AND AUTOBIOGRAPHY

Talking
Open House
Apes and Angels
Midnight on the Desert
Rain upon Godshill
The Secret Dream

Delight
All About Ourselves and other Essays
  (chosen by Eric Gillett)
Thoughts in the Wilderness
Margin Released
The Moments and other pieces

CRITICISM AND MISCELLANEOUS

Brief Diversions
The English Comic Characters
Meredith (E.M.L.)
Peacock (E.M.L.)
The English Novel
English Humour (Heritage Series)
The Balconinny
English Journey
Postscripts
Out of the People
British Women Go To War
Russian Journey

Theatre Outlook
The Olympians (opera libretto)
Journey Down a Rainbow (with Jacquetta
  Hawkes)
Topside
The Art of the Dramatist
Literature and Western Man
Man and Time
The World of J. B. Priestley (edited by
  Donald G. MacRae)
Trumpets over the Sea

TRUMPETS
OVER THE SEA

*Being a rambling and egotistical account of
The London Symphony Orchestra's engagement
at Daytona Beach, Florida, in July-August, 1967*

J. B. PRIESTLEY

HEINEMANN : LONDON

William Heinemann Ltd.
LONDON MELBOURNE TORONTO
CAPE TOWN AUCKLAND

Printed in Great Britain by
Morrison and Gibb Ltd., London and Edinburgh

DEDICATED

---

*Out of gratitude, admiration and
affection to the Directors and members
of the London Symphony Orchestra*

CONTENTS

PRELUDE—*agitato*   1

FIRST MOVEMENT—*ad libitum*   18

SECOND MOVEMENT—*allegro moderato*   43

THIRD MOVEMENT—*poco allegretto*   74

FOURTH MOVEMENT—*poco a poco bizzaramente*   102

FINALE—*tema con varazione—tutti*   136

The illustrations are arranged in two sections, the first between pages 32 and 33, and the second between pages 96 and 97.

"A few of the photographs are included here by courtesy of the *Daytona Beach News Journal.* The rest were taken by my wife. J.B.P."

Prelude

agitato

EARLY on the evening of Sunday, 9th July (the year being 1967), I arrived at a most disturbing conclusion: I had made a fool of myself, and on a large and expensive scale too. I was then sitting in an upstairs room, obviously a boy's bedroom, of a furnished house that I had taken for a month, paying the rent in advance. I was up there because that room alone had an air-conditioning unit that was working properly, not only lowering the temperature but, what was more important, reducing the humidity. (An expert told me, the following day, that when he installed a big air-conditioning unit in a Daytona Beach house he expected to take out of it in the first two days between *sixty and seventy gallons of water*— yes, simply out of the curtains, carpets, clothes, walls!) My wife, Jacquetta, and I had been to places equally warm and wet, places like Darwin, Bangkok, Singapore, Lima, but there at least we had not been compelled to install ourselves in a house that was not ready for us. After nearly forty-eight hours of it, Jacquetta was pretending hard that she was not in despair. To spend a month at this Florida Music Festival, to rent a furnished house at Daytona Beach and bring to it, flying across the Atlantic with the orchestra and its wives and children, partly to help us, partly as a holiday lark, our household from Kissing Tree House, Alveston, had never been her idea—she had been swept here by a rising tide of male grandeur and folly—and now, having changed my shirt for the fourth time that day, I was up in that room, fairly cool but brooding over my idiocy, wondering what the devil I thought

1]

I was doing there, while she was grilling steak in a kitchen that was equally busy grilling her. And there could be no giving it up, hurrying back to the New York we had left on Friday, because somewhere in the air were three excited women, long settled in our employment, wondering how soon they would join us. I had wished it and now I was stuck with it.

On Friday evening, arriving from New York via Atlanta, we had been rather cursorily greeted by the President of the Festival, Mr Tippen Davidson, with whom I had corresponded, and then I was immediately photographed with Itzhak Perlman, the Israeli violinist, who had come on the same plane. Our landlord had hastily shown us the house and some of the neighbouring shops. After that—nothing. Nobody called or rang up to bid us welcome. Nobody suggested a meal or even a drink. Later, amid much hospitality, we learnt that people hadn't wished—it is their term—'to intrude'. But any such intrusion would have delighted us. There we were, sweating away—the general air-conditioning having broken down at once—in a strange house not really ready for us. We had no car—a necessity in any place like Daytona Beach—because we had arranged for our secretary, who would do most of our driving, to hire a car on Monday morning. So, carless, we trudged and sweated, carrying large brown-paper bags of this and that, Jacquetta making sure we had something to eat and I making equally sure—for by Heaven we needed it—we had something to drink. I didn't propose to drown my folly, but we certainly needed a little booze to cushion us against the rasp of reality—if this *was* reality.

Not having rented a furnished house for many years, I had forgotten that as soon as you did acquire one you moved at once into the world of old *Punch* articles and slapstick films. But here we were again. We turned on a shower upstairs and water gushed through a hole in the dining-room ceiling. We would open a cupboard and start an avalanche of children's broken toys and old clothes. Drawers were so full they could

[2

hardly be opened. Doors that ought to have locked wouldn't stay closed, and other doors that ought to have opened freely couldn't be budged. And—the gags getting cornier and staler —I even found myself hammering on a bathroom door because I couldn't let myself out. The man who came to plaster over the hole in the dining-room ceiling turned out to be a very pleasant fellow, but even he in his white overalls had a custard-pie look about him. Men came and went all day, chiefly to stare at the failed air-conditioning plant, but though they arrived apparently full of American technology and know-how, brisk and hopeful, somehow they all turned vague, gave us dreamy replies, then faded away like ghosts. At any moment, it seemed, Buster Keaton might have been attending to us. No doubt all this could have added up to what they might call round there *a fun thing*. But it didn't. And not because the typewriter I hired on Saturday morning was altogether too new, progressive, up-to-the-minute, though it was, being cluttered with various 'magical' devices that did nothing but confuse me: I want a typewriter for authorship, not conjuring. Nor because I found myself steaming down there in the kitchen, merely after squeezing two limes into a glass; or after going through those cupboards containing everything from tins of instant mashed potatoes to smelly concoctions of roach paste, everything, that is, except what I looked for in vain—common salt. Not even discovering—a final irony—that our one air-conditioning unit that worked, up in the boy's room, soon began to seem too cold. No, no, no— what killed any *fun thing* nonsense by the time it was Sunday evening was one brief and brutal question, to which I could find no adequate reply. *What the devil did I think I was doing?*

(Here I must add that later that evening I felt better, even though the question remained unanswered. This was because Mary and Henry McLemore, who lived across the road, decided to 'intrude' and asked us in for a drink. And we all took to one another, and, after meeting on many occasions, we

3]

spent our very last night in Florida with them. Instead of being compact and aggressive, Mary McLemore is tall, rather vague, her voice often floating away, and charming; and after years in Europe she had sent herself back to college, at least by day, and was taking some mysterious degree in English. And Henry was exactly the kind of American I like; an old newspaperman and a sardonic wit, who had begun as a cub sports writer in the great days of Ring Lardner and Grantland Rice and was now a syndicated columnist. No other pair in Daytona suited us as well as they did, and it was a fine piece of luck to have them as neighbours. So the evening ended more cheerfully, but I was still asking myself what I thought I was doing.)

Broadly speaking I would call myself a rather indolent and self-indulgent man, deficient in will-power and any determination to succeed all round, to make the very best of myself. In one matter alone do I show—and have long shown—a certain obstinacy and an independence of mind and spirit. I decide for myself what I shall work at, and I hang on to the chosen task like a bulldog. But from the first—and this was why I felt uneasy and depressed—with this Daytona Beach idea I had blown hot and cold. And now that I was here, a hell of a long way from anywhere I wanted to be, while I was hot I was also blowing cold, like that boy's-room air-conditioner in the steamy night. Was I or wasn't I making a gigantic and expensive fool of myself?

[4

2

It was some time during the autumn of 1966 when the idea first raised its fantastic head, out of a loch of print. I had been reading a good many accounts of the engagement by the Florida International Music Festival of the London Symphony Orchestra. (And to save time, space and temper, from now on the former will be referred to simply as the *Festival*, the latter as the *L.S.O.* or *the orchestra*.) Of these many accounts I will quote only one, from *Time* magazine, chiefly because it is not British and biased but American:

> 'It is so mad, so utterly wild a scheme that we can't resist!' So saying, the management of the London Symphony canceled 20 recording sessions, five concerts, refused an invitation to the Athens Festival and, with the abandon of undergrads leaving for spring vacation, bundled the orchestra off to that big sandbox in the sun, Daytona Beach, Fla. They are the attraction at the first Florida International Music Festival, by far the most culturally ambitious festival in the Southeast.
>
> Scheduled for a month-long stay, the London Symphony is the first European orchestra to settle in a U.S. city for such an extended engagement. When they arrived two weeks ago—96 musicians, 43 wives and 36 children—they were met by a caravan of 40 cars and treated to a wee-hour spin across Daytona's famed beach. In the days since, it has been one continuous round of sun and surf—and great music.

Now apart from the Edinburgh Festival, which is too big—I prefer a one-ring to a three-ring circus—I am all in favour of festivals. I have had some modest connection with several, ran my own chamber music festival for ten years in the Isle of Wight, and the longest novel I have published so far is called *Festival at Farbridge*. Moreover, I liked the counter-punching in this Daytona enterprise. Some intelligent people over there wanted to attack its 'sex, suds and sand' reputation. They were tired of their town, as a resort, being associated in the public mind only with speed trials, college boys swarming in for jazz jamborees on the sand and 'naked girls being bounced on a beach blanket'. So let there be music, even if it must be enjoyed in the steamy height of summer! And good luck to them, I thought.

But there was something else, below even this rather low level of rationality. The wildness of the scheme, the sheer daftness of it—as if Margate or Great Yarmouth had engaged the Philadelphia or Boston Symphony for a month—appealed to me just as it had done to the L.S.O. management. And if they could do something daft, then why shouldn't I? If they could fly over the sea a hundred men and some of their wives and children and all their instruments and music—about the equivalent of putting a herd of elephants into the air—why shouldn't I rent a Daytona furnished house for a month—no going alone and staying in an hotel I could leave any time—and take this whole Alveston household there? And this was not altogether daft. I had long been interested in symphonic orchestras and the men who played in them. (I began a novel about one, twenty years ago, but there were too many characters—even for me.) And I had often wanted to observe an orchestra at close quarters, impossible to do in London, where the men are either hard at work or scattered in homes forty miles apart. Again, I had always had some favourite orchestra. An age ago it had been the London Philharmonic; then, some years after the war it had been the Philharmonia, created by the redoubtable and fairly ruthless Walter Legge; and now it was the L.S.O., risen like a Phoenix, with its principals so many virtuosi and its back desks crammed with eager and tireless youth, combining precision and delicacy with a fiery magnificence. And I knew already, from various reports, that in Daytona Beach the L.S.O. had not only triumphantly given a number of symphony concerts (and it is very much a triumphant orchestra), it had lent its virtuosi to chamber music; it had taken on classes of students from

[6

neighbouring universities; and, together with its wives and children, almost at once it had found a welcome and warm place in the life of the local community. So it was not altogether a daft idea.

But Florida in the height of summer? And a furnished house and a household flown three thousand miles? And only a book could justify all this trouble and expense—and how did I know, sitting in Alveston, Warwickshire, there was a book in it? So I decided to take both my idea and my doubts about it to the General Secretary of the L.S.O., Ernest Fleischmann. And though the torch I tossed may have been only smouldering, it landed in a hundred gallons of petrol.

3

Even now, after much talk about it, I don't know how good
or bad Ernest Fleischmann's management of an orchestra can
be. But as an enthusiastic and persuasive salesman he is in the
highest class. In half an hour he had me blowing hot. (But it
wouldn't have worked, I think, if I hadn't liked him
personally.) The L.S.O. of course was wonderful, unequalled
anywhere; the Festival at Daytona was wonderful; my idea was
wonderful. If he had offered me a furnished house then and
there—and I gathered they would be two a penny—I would
have taken it. He made me feel ashamed of any doubts I may
have had, and indeed I dared not bring them out to wither in
the furnace of his enthusiasm. I am not sure now if I risked a
question about the summer climate of Florida's east coast, but
I do remember that he told me that the temperature was no
more than eighty-five degrees, cooled by pleasant sea breezes.
And he was not trying to deceive me, though in fact he had
not spent the whole month out there and anyhow was himself a
South African, whose idea of a hottish day could probably
give mine about fifteen degrees. No, no, his natural zest and
enthusiasm were too busy adding one glowing hue after
another to the picture of me and the L.S.O. and Daytona
Beach, a glittering tableau with full brass and percussion.

Subsequent meetings only added strings and woodwind and
a touch of intoxication. Just as most people find going behind
the scenes in the Theatre a heady experience—and I don't
after working there for twenty-five years—so I never feel
quite sober when taken into the world, so rich in its magic,
of professional and highly accomplished musicians. Once in
there I abolish all critical standards (though not at Daytona,
as we shall see), to gape and wonder. And Ernest Fleischmann,
sizzling and almost incandescent, began to make me feel I was

[8

about to join the orchestra, not to conduct it but perhaps to act as principal of a new pen-and-typewriter section. New recordings came my way; a box for the next concert and a very pleasant supper-party afterwards; and I stared with respect at schedules of rehearsals, recordings, concerts, that arrived by post as if I were already *one of them*. No doubts now about the Daytona idea. I was impatient for the months to pass. Did I blow hot? I was on fire.

But then—and not because I am getting on, turning unreliable, unstable—the doubts began to creep back. Where, for example, were the furnished houses I had been told could be had for the asking? I didn't know, and now, it seemed, nor did Tippen Davidson, with whom I had been exchanging letters. But this was nothing compared with a further blow—a left hook out of the blue. Suddenly, without the least hint of a warning, there was no Ernest Fleischmann. He had left the L.S.O. My anchor-man had gone; the fire was out. (Later, when he was already busy with another job, he could still express—at long-distance telephone rates too—his unbated enthusiasm for the orchestra itself.) Player-directors like Barry Tuckwell and Michael Winfield were ready to answer the kind of questions I had been putting to Ernest Fleischmann, but after all they were rehearsing or recording nearly every day and performing almost every night, and I felt I ought not to be a nuisance. I began to feel dubious again. A suitable house (though in fact it wasn't) had been found for me; arrangements were going forward, both at Alveston and Daytona; I was already signing documents for the bank to prove I was fit to have an allowance of dollars; but in all this I was now playing my part mechanically, without any surge and glow in my inner world. The temperature went down and down; I was blowing cold now. And a casual chat with an American publisher, who said he couldn't imagine anybody living at Daytona Beach ever reading a book, fed me no heat.

Zero was in sight when I agreed to speak for a minute or

two to the orchestra. I went without hope, as many other people must have done, to Walthamstow Town Hall. This astonishing rendezvous came out of the exigencies of recording: the L.S.O., under Boulez, was doing some pieces by Webern. After listening to some gloomy and disconnected sounds, which had to be repeated several times, though I could never detect any difference in their performance, I was able to make use of a tea break and speak my own little piece. It was no triumph of oratory but at least it was not as gloomy and disconnected as Webern-Boulez had been. And then, after talking to some of the musicians in and outside the hall and later over lunch, I found myself blowing hot again. The idea was *on*. I was ready and eager again for that month in Florida. The men themselves did it. I had often heard them play like triumphant spirits, but I have lived long enough to know that some men can do that and yet be damnably disagreeable once their instruments are back in their cases. ('The trouble there,' said Fleischmann when we were talking about a famous American orchestra, 'is they're such a lot of bastards.') But all the L.S.O. men I met that morning in Walthamstow were so unaffectedly cheerful, friendly, welcoming and hopeful, that the temperature went shooting up. And I will add here, for the record, that if I liked them as a body of men in Walthamstow, I liked them even more after we shared this month in Florida. If they are not exceptionally pleasant, open-hearted, zestful men, good company anywhere, then they are not only fine musicians but better actors than can be found in the National Theatre. Anyhow, after Walthamstow, though I hadn't a notion about what kind of book I might be able to write (and I had already refused some invitations to serialize pieces of it), and in spite of the fuss about dollars and packing and all the arrangements, I still regarded my idea with favour, even fervour.

Perhaps it was a mistake to go a week earlier than anybody else and to spend most of that week in New York, even though

[10

we had old friends to see and some business to discuss. New York took me down a few pegs. I lose my enthusiasm for anything in that city. For years now it has had for me a strongly negative influence. W. H. Auden, who lives there and loves it, has declared that in his view it is the only city in the world that isn't provincial. So if I say I dislike the place, he can retort that that is because I am essentially provincial. And perhaps I am, but this argument won't work. In the thirties, though still afraid of New York, I felt its power, its boldness, its glamour: it was still 'the enfabled rock' of Tom Wolfe's novel. But ever since then it has been slithering downhill. It is increasingly dirty and sour. There may be a few fine new buildings and Lincoln Center, but it has lost most of its newspapers and the restaurants I liked best; its Theatre is a shambles; most of its art is either borrowed or bogus; it is appallingly expensive, making you pay more and more for less and less; and, worst of all, now as a mere expense-account metropolis it has lost for ever the character, like that of a wine once rich and dry, that it still had when I first went there and that belonged to the *World* newspaper and the earlier *New Yorker* and Mencken and Nathan and the Marx Brothers and Joe Cook and the older hotels and clubs as well as *Jack and Charley's*. Cosmopolitan it may be, if only to please Auden, but it is crammed with assorted types who want to give as little as possible and take as much as they can in order to get out of the goddam place. No other big city offers you fewer people of genuine talent, simply because such people now prefer to live and work somewhere else. Over tall highballs that merely freeze the stomach and never illuminate the mind, the fifth-rate yap and yap about the recent doings of the third-rate. You are still asked if you can stand the bustle and pace when in fact you are increasingly appalled by the slowness of everybody and everything. (Lack of sleep and too much noise account for much of this.) Even the vast buildings now look as if they were the creation of giants who departed shrugging, years ago. It is now the capital city of admen and press agents, the rag trade, dealers in forged pictures and faked antiques, famed continental restaurateurs who only carried trays in Nice, ticket scalpers for mechanical 'smash hits', visiting firemen, out-of-town buyers living it up on salesmen's expense accounts, and tourists ridding themselves of illusions. If I am being too severe, that is probably because I paid the equivalent of £15 a night for a smallish bedroom and bathroom and, when not being entertained by friends at home, never had a decent meal. Moreover, in the atmosphere of New York it was impossible for even our friends to believe there was any sense in our spending a month in a torrid honky-tonk like Daytona Beach. And for that first forty-eight hours I fancied they were right.

4

New York can take it, but I must try to be fair to Daytona
Beach, even if I never found a single bookshop there. (Paper-
backs abounded, of course, all *explosive, stark, searing,* but an
author trying to be reasonable between hard covers was about
as much in demand as an alchemist or a lecturer in Hegelian
metaphysics.) To begin with, it was not as honky-tonky as I
had imagined it would be. I had known worse—in Southern
California and Australia's 'Gold Coast' running between New
South Wales and Queensland, and indeed, for brutally
determined ugliness, some stretches of England's south-east
coast. Daytona Beach proper, as distinct from the large
metropolitan area with a population of about 100,000, is a long
narrow strip of a resort between the ocean and the wide
Halifax river. On each side of its Atlantic Avenue are hotels
and motels, over four hundred altogether, and they have names
like *Capri, Corsair, Desert Isle, Grand Prix, Hawaiian Inn, Isle
of Palms, Monte Carlo, New Frontier, Oceanfront Villas, Pelican
Shoals, Pleasure Isle, Spindrift Cottages, Suez* (God knows why),
Sunglow, Tropical Manor Motel, and *Voyager Beach Motel,* this
last an enormous place, both air-conditioned and heated, and
offering 'efficiencies' (whatever they are) '4 pools, putting
green, shuffleboard, TV, radio, golf privileges, restaurant and
lounge and entertainment'. The architecture and general
décor of this bewildering array were as fancy dictated with
perhaps some help from Disneyland. Summer tourists,
largely drawn from Atlanta and other south-eastern cities, can
also enjoy speedway trials, dog racing at the Kennel Club,
Jal Alai (a form of pelota), golf and bridge tournaments,
various forms of entertainment, and in one week alone, that of
the *Annual Dixie Frolics Pageant with Beauty Contestants from
all the Southern States competing for the Miss Dixie Title,* there

13]

would be Fashion Shows, Street Dances, Sailing Regatta, Fishing Derby, Surfing Meet, a Beach Parade, Fireworks, Golf Tournament and the Hound Dog Derby. Imagine turning up here with a Bach Partita, Brahms's Horn Trio or Bartok's *Bluebeard's Castle*! There are some brave men behind that Florida International Music Festival.

The famous beach itself, very long, very broad, and mostly composed of hard-packed dazzling sand, has a lot of shallow water and so is perfect for family bathing, though swimming far out where the undertow begins can be dangerous, so that there are lifeguards at regular intervals. I am not a beach man myself. Going into the sea, coming out to slap on suntan oil, going in again, coming out again, dozing in the shade of a cabaña, all this seems tedious to me; and our remote ancestors, though well adapted to the life after a few million years of it, did well to make at last for the land. But there was a certain fascination to the eye in the long dimming vistas of sand and tide, set below skies of cerulean and even cobalt blue with a few clouds of solid titanium white, and I tried a few *gouache* sketches, which are not too bad. But as I refuse to paint motorcars, there had to be much deliberate elimination, for this beach, which in fact ranks as a state highway, is as thick with cars as any High Street, cars on the move, if slowly, and cars parked in rows. Antics with cars on the beach, I understand, form the central attraction of the college boys' jamborees at Daytona, but I think the rest of us, no longer intoxicated by our youth, would have been better off if the automobile had never been allowed to invade the beach. And many Americans would be healthier if now and again they had to walk a few hundred yards.

I will admit that during the first morning, when I tried walking along the beach, partly in the hope of running into some L.S.O. family parties, I found it hot and heavy going. I remember floundering, already wet through, to one of the kiosks, which sell cold fruit drinks, ice cream, hot dogs and

[14

pickles, to ask for a large orange juice. The small girl in front
of me—it was about eleven o'clock with the shade temperature
in the nineties—was buying hot dogs and pickles but then
said: 'You got any French fries?' And she wasn't English, of
course, putting the question that way; even our chips-with-
everything countrymen would have been happy to go without
them, at that hour and sweltering on that beach. Though I
must add that more often that not—this particular morning
being an exception—the Atlantic stirred the air and brought
down its temperature.

The best sketch I did of the beach was rather small and
had to be done quickly. This was because a thunderstorm was
coming up from the south, and even the first spatter of rain
would spoil my paper. The sea was pale green against the
sepia and indigo of the thickening sky, but even though the
sun had gone, the sand and the dunes and the coloured
façades of the motels in the distance took on a luminous
quality; and some of this I caught—or so I imagine. These
thunderstorms arrived nearly every afternoon and at first I
welcomed them, partly because they brought with them swift
and immensely dramatic effects, also because they cooled the
air. But after a week or so, as we shall discover, they became a
bore, especially when they rolled round for hours, like Wagner
going on too long, and darkened and drenched everything.
For the rest it was bright sunlight of a kind I never really
enjoyed; after early morning there was no freshness in it; and I
had only to walk a mile or so, not among the supermarkets and
motels of Atlantic Avenue but along parallel and dull avenues,
to soak my clothes in sweat. The short cross-streets, Seabreeze
and Broadway and the rest, had the shops, but apart from a
grocer's trying hard to be different, they were not interesting.
Over the bridges and across the river, in the other Daytona,
the shops were better but still no great shakes. It was on that
side, not far from the river, where one found the older
bungalows, hiding among trees and having an old Deep

15]

South plantation air about them. Such houses mostly belonged to retired folk, who had come to Florida to escape the least breath of winter, and this may have been equally true of the newer houses on our side, the Beach side, where there were several long avenues between the honky-tonkery tourism of Atlantic Avenue and the wide silent river. All these houses had unfenced gardens of a sort, cared for but with few flowers and a peculiar grass that always looked to me as if it had come from a factory; but occasionally there was the crimson flash of a cardinal bird, and an enormous yellow butterfly sometimes visited us, though for what purpose I cannot imagine. Most of these retired householders were not concert-goers; they had retired from everything except food and drink, golf and bridge and *Bonanza* on TV.

Clearly the climate slowed them down and enabled them to live a long time, after retreating from the blizzards, sales charts, and coronaries of the North. Its effect upon me—and perhaps I am slipping in an apology for what follows in later chapters—was to turn my brains into a mush, not unlike the *grits* of a Deep South breakfast. Sustained work was impossible, and, oddly enough, the chances of it did not improve but got worse. I did contrive to write a few pages during the first horrible forty-eight hours, when I was wondering if I had made a fool of myself (perhaps working out of sheer desperation), but as the lotus afternoons went sliding past I had to force myself to the typewriter to produce a few lines of notes, just memory-jogging stuff; and then would retreat, usually in search of a drink, as if I had just been digging the Panama Canal. Everybody else seemed much the same—with one astounding and glorious exception—the musicians. There they were until the very end, bang on the beat, not missing a note. Many of them would be up at dawn for an early bathe, would rehearse all morning, be back on the beach, perhaps for a 'shrimp boil' or out fishing, in the afternoon, play in the evening, live it up at parties until the small hours; and yet at

[16

eleven o'clock on the very last night be knocking hell out of the finale of Dvorak's Sixth Symphony. And even now, when my brains are no longer a mush, I still cannot understand how they did it. There must be something life-enhancing and life-giving in music itself—consider the master-conductors who stand up there waving their arms until they are ninety—so that Ponce de Leon, who came to Florida looking for the Fountain of Youth, would have done better to stay at home with viols and sackbuts and polyphony. There will be moments recorded here when I felt I might be catching a glimpse of that Fountain of Youth; but I was never allowed a taste of its waters. Otherwise, what follows would reach a finer quality— or perhaps not exist at all.

First Movement

ad libitum

Now that the L.S.O. had dropped down from the sky
—about a hundred men, forty-six wives, fifty-three
children, two tons of instruments, music, baggage—I went
poking around the Peabody Auditorium, where for the next
four weeks we would hear the music. It was much better than
I expected it to be. It was built in the early fifties on the site
of an earlier wooden hall, and unfortunately this act of piety
deprived the new building of any adequate parking facilities, a
lack that condemned us all to a lot of waiting about before the
month was out. It is wide, cool, and comfortable, with one
large balcony, to complete a capacity of about 2,500, and has
a civilized décor in various oceanic shades of green and blue,
to remind one that the sea is almost round the corner. The
floor is slightly raked so that in the best seats in the middle (at
$10 a head—a stiff price for a small seaside town) you are
more or less on a level with the orchestra, though for my part—
and looking a gift horse hard in the mouth—I would have
preferred to have been given seats in the front row of the
balcony, offering better sight and sound. The trouble here was
that this Peabody Auditorium had not been designed primarily
as a concert hall. Instead of an open platform, on which an
orchestra could be built up and given plenty of room, it has a
proscenium stage, exceptionally wide but very shallow, and,
even so, not wide enough to accommodate a full symphony
orchestra, with the result that the back desks of the first
violins, on one side, and the second row of the double basses,
on the other side, seemed to be almost in the wings. Another

[18

snag, which I pointed out at once, without anybody telling me to mind my own business, was that the superb L.S.O. woodwind, instead of being above the strings, merely sat behind them on the same level, so that they were not to be seen from the floor and often, during fortissimo passages, could hardly be heard, caught as they were between the fiercely aggressive L.S.O. strings and the magnificent brass above them. I still feel this could have been remedied, by the addition of a few more rostrums, but it never was.

To see for the first time this aristocrat of orchestras rehearsing there was an odd experience. It was as if—to see but not to hear—a band of sorts had been hastily collected, perhaps press-ganged, from any sub-tropical seashore. One stared at bare legs, sandals, shorts, beach coats, bathing costumes, anything that would pass on the shore. It was hard to believe that Handel, Beethoven, Brahms, solemn and thickly-clothed Germans, writing to be heard on cold nights, could recognizably emerge from such frivolous motley. This first sight of the undressed orchestra—and after a day or two I took it for granted—offered me a not unwelcome return, after my various dubieties, to the original wild daftness of the whole idea.

The Auditorium foyer seemed ample enough at first sight, but proved to be inadequate later for the half-hour intermissions of the major concerts, when it was heatedly jammed with people trying to drink Coca-cola out of cardboard tumblers. There was, it turned out, a fair-sized refreshment room to the right of this foyer, where snacks were served during the intermissions, but not a drink was to be had even there. This barbarous puritanical ban, which casts its shadow over so many halls, theatres, colleges in America, not only robbed Jacquetta and me of civilized refreshment but also deprived the Festival of profits that might have amounted to several thousand dollars it badly needed. And let nobody tell me I exaggerate for there were to be concerts here, major or minor, for almost every night for a month, and I knew from personal experience what profits the bars of one small London theatre could earn. And here there were far more people, thirstier people too, and half-hour intermissions on warm nights. Besides, quite apart from the money that was being lost, Coca-cola and coffee are not the proper accompaniments to Handel, Beethoven and Brahms. It is time America realized that there is a civilized middle way between *Not a drop of liquor here!* and the *Come right in and get stoned, man!* of ten thousand dimly lit bars.

This foyer was the headquarters of the Festival Hospitality Committee, where a few Daytona matrons and their handsome daughters—and as usual the real work was left to a few— toiled to make the men of the L.S.O. and their wives feel they were welcomed and cared-for, making lists of hostesses and providers of entertainment and even noting down the special interests of their English visitors, from amberjack fishing to the moon rockets at neighbouring Cape Kennedy. But though the Press, after the first year, had declared that the whole of Daytona had opened its houses, pockets and hearts to the L.S.O., I soon discovered that this was not true. A large section, probably an easy majority, caring nothing about music, neither attended the concerts nor welcomed the musicians. The attendance, the hospitality, the entertainment, all came from a comparatively small but very enthusiastic group, most of whom were progressive and liberal in their political views and were far removed from the imbecilities of the John Birch Society, which has its adherents among the hazy dim-wits of Florida. These more advanced though hardly radical views belong also to the two local papers, the *Daytona Beach Morning* and *Evening* journals, which are managed—it is a family concern, going back three generations—by Tippen Davidson, himself the President and chief ball-of-fire of the Festival, who before returning to newspaper publishing had studied music at Juilliard. He is an enthusiast, obviously intelligent and

sensitive, and I took to him as a correspondent. But as we discovered when we dined with him and his amiable and helpful
wife, that first Monday night, he is much easier to correspond
with than to talk to, being one of those hard-pressed men who
keep darting away to make telephone calls, and, even while
restraining themselves to sit at the table for a few minutes,
somehow give the impression that they are impatiently
awaiting long-distance messages far more important than
anything you could ever tell them. Indeed, there were moments
that night when I began to feel I was in a film about some
underground revolutionary movement, probably in Mexico,
and that a Chief of Police might soon arrest us all. After that,
though we had plenty to talk about, I doubt if I exchanged half
a dozen sentences with this enthusiastic President of the
Festival, and concluded that either he was very shy or didn't
like the look of me. For that matter, I never liked the look of
myself in Daytona, for in the numerous, far too numerous,
photographs (no fault of mine) that found their way into Mr
Davidson's morning and evening journals, I always looked like
something between Goering and a quack doctor.

2

On this Wednesday, 12th July, the Second Florida International Music Festival opened at Peabody Auditorium. It was very much a social occasion, and there were plenty of people outside—

To see the great ones and the rich
And those that only pose as sich.

In the ten-dollar seats, our ladies turned themselves into hot-house flowers, and we men wore our dinner jackets, tuxedos, *soup-and-fish*. There was an audience of about two thousand, a thirty per cent increase, I was told, on last year's opening attendance. At first the orchestra was not to be seen, only its music stands and chairs and some flags hanging on the wall behind. There were some speeches, short and painless: a brief announcement from Tippen Davidson; then a nice little speech from Paul Wright, head of British Information in the U.S. (the British Council does not operate in this country), and able for once to speak in all sincerity because he is a musician himself and is genuinely proud of the L.S.O.; and finally some official statements from the Florida Secretary of State, who told us that 'the Festival has attracted international acclaim and focused attention on Daytona Beach and Florida'. Then the musicians came swarming in, looking cool and natty in white shirts, black dress trousers and black sashes and bow ties, their faces already browned or reddened by the sun. (The tympanist, high at the back, was a boiled lobster.) And as they took their places, I remember wondering, believing as I do that a lot of sun makes one feel stupid, how long it would be before entrances would be missed and significant notes strangled or otherwise botched; and I had a disturbing vision—never realized, praise the Lord!—of a

[22

boiled-lobster L.S.O., towards the end of the month, taking an extra quarter of an hour over each symphony.

The leader, John Georgiadis, a handsome young man leading a large number of other handsome young men (the average age of the L.S.O. is thirty-three, and most of the first fiddles are younger than that), made his delayed entrance, following the custom originated by Reed, many years ago, when he was leader of the L.S.O. I grudge nothing to concert masters but I rather deplore this custom, if only because it is an unnecessary hold-up, lengthening the time between our settling down to listen and the actual start of the music. Then of course came the conductor of this opening concert, Istvan Kertesz, making his first appearance here. Succeeding Pierre Monteux as principal conductor of the L.S.O. must have been heart-shaking to a man half a century younger, like trying on the shoes of an ancient giant; but I was glad to notice that Kertesz, who had seemed more boyish than his thirty-six years when I had talked to him the night before, now immediately took on age and authority as he faced the audience and then the orchestra. A chubby and cheerful Hungarian, he has almost a chubby and cheerful beat. He gave us the *Star Spangled Banner* and *God Save the Queen* (good but not equal to Beecham's, which always made me feel we had all just rescued the monarch from some desperate peril); together with the sound of those tremendous and triumphant L.S.O. cymbals, which end high in the air like new suns. Then, all the nonsense over, the music began.

In a piece about the Festival in the *New York Times*, sent to me by a friend, Allen Hughes complained that this opening programme 'could hardly have been more hackneyed'. But music critics attend too many concerts and never try running expensive festivals in places like Daytona Beach. In point of fact it was a very good opening programme and far better balanced than most of those that came later: the Handel-Harty *Water Music*; the Beethoven Fourth Piano Concerto,

23]

played by 'the artist in residence', Ashkenazy; and the Brahms First Symphony in C Minor. Certainly all three are familiar enough to most of us, but that does not mean they are hackneyed, each of them richly representing its own period and each a masterpiece in its own kind. (Besides, as Neville Cardus likes to declare: 'There are no hackneyed masterpieces, only hackneyed listeners and hackneyed music critics.') A person new to serious music could begin to enjoy these works while others who have heard them many times, as I have, could listen to them again without boredom. After running my own chamber music festival for ten years, I know about choosing programmes, so I blow a rude noise in the direction of Allen Hughes and the *New York Times*.

I neither know nor care how much of the *Water Music*, as we hear it now, is Handel and how much Hamilton Harty. But the L.S.O. made a delicious *smörgasbord* out of it. The virtuosi were with us, Handel-wise or Harty-wise. As the ravishing second movement, the *Air*, went trailing and fading, as if taking something away for ever, I thought how music doesn't interpret history but the eternal myths that are at once above and below history. One of them, suggested here, is that of the other and better time, the lost golden age. When American scientists and technologists describe, as they are so fond of doing, the marvels of the year 2000, most of us over eighteen feel dubious and cold. No myth begins to glow in the darkness of the mind. But though I would hate to be suddenly transported to the England of George I, a brutal age, under the spell of its *Water Music* and the orchestra it becomes for a moment a fabled Avalon and I seem to catch a glimpse of the unfading apple blossom.

Ashkenazy appeared, almost apologetically, to play the Beethoven No. 4. He has an odd platform manner for a concert pianist who, though still young, is already world-renowned. He is small and silent and shy—sparing of talk, like his blonde Icelandic-London wife—but his diffident appearance masks

[24

formidable resources of will, determination, personality. His performance of the concerto left Allen Hughes of the *New York Times* deeply offended: 'It may be,' he concluded, anger melting into sorrow, 'that Mr Ashkenazy will reconsider some of his ideas or at least string them together in a more convincing statement.' I couldn't support this rebuke, though the relation between the soloist and the orchestra was not always happy. Though he has exiled himself from the U.S.S.R., partly because it exercises too strict a control over the artists it sends abroad, Ashkenazy brings from Gorky, where he was born, and Moscow, where he was trained, a certain Russianness of spirit, melancholy and melting and yet fiery, that makes many essentially German compositions, like this Fourth Concerto, sound new and strange. There is much to be said for Slavs playing Germans and Germans playing Slavs—a kind of European balance being achieved. Now this Fourth happens to be my favourite Beethoven piano concerto, but on an off-night it can be rather a sleepy or tinkly job. And Ashkenazy wasn't having any of that. He could be infinitely delicate and tender—and was rewarded in the slow movement by a number of coughs from the social-occasion customers—but where too many pianists begin to sound bored, as if the work were too long and they had played it too often, Ashkenazy kindled and blazed. Taken all round it seemed to me a splendidly unusual performance, and I for one would have liked less noise while it was on and more noise after its conclusion. It was well received but with no shouts of joyous gratitude, no metropolitan thunder of applause. Perhaps Allen Hughes was already at work on them.

There was now the half-hour intermission, too long for a hall without a bar. Everybody except the Priestleys took to cardboard and Coca-cola. But not all were Daytona socialites dedicated to a gala occasion. There were some youngsters, probably from the Festival Institute (of which, more later) and the neighbouring Stetson University, in whom the music was still bubbling like yeast. And a woman from out of town was heard to declare: 'I worked all year to come for these weeks.' That is the woman who should make a speech at next year's opening, and never mind the Director of This and Secretary of That: she and her kind are at the root of this matter. And while billions of dollars are taken from them in taxes to put some men on the moon, a mere small fraction of these would bring the moon, still shining in glory, to them.

Next, after the audience had settled down, and then and later I never knew an audience that took longer to settle down, we had the Brahms C Minor. I have been listening to this great symphony off and on for nearly sixty years, and I wrote about it, after a novelist's fashion, nearly forty years ago in *Angel Pavement*. And now I shall disagree with Allen Hughes again. (But for the last time; we are about to say Goodbye.) To him all was well here in the Brahms—a straightforward interpretation—unequivocal in expressive intent—nicely balanced instrumentality—that kind of thing. But while in New York the Brahms C Minor may be a nice piece of music, to my mind it should represent a challenging tragic experience. And Kertesz turned it into so much mellowness—a vista of autumnal fields and woods—beautiful sound. (And he did it again, at the repeat performance on the Saturday night.) And with this orchestra the beautiful sound was all too easy. In the middle movements, where the tragic experience is held up, waiting for the finale, we were delicately and delightfully handed from one master instrumentalist to another, from Barry Tuckwell's horn to Gervase de Peyer's clarinet to Roger Lord's oboe and so on. All very fine. Kertesz is an excellent musician and in this orchestra he has a superb instrument, responsive to every flicker of baton or hand. But I couldn't help remembering the last performance (disregarding recordings) I had heard of this noble work, when at the Royal Festival Hall Klemperer and the Philharmonia, then at its height, had moved from Beethoven to Brahms. From the very

[26

beginning, with the tremendous tympany and its strokes of doom, Klemperer announced that he had terrible news for us. Man was to be heated in the furnace, hammered, shaped anew. Brahms had pushed aside his liver sausage and roast goose to thump the table, to glare at us, to warn us. And Klemperer, the stricken colossus, to whom everything had happened but the defeat of the spirit, was up there with him, to the last brazen cry of anguish, the final triumphant chords. The difference in interpretation is the difference between two opposing types of men: Kertesz, young, hearty, euphoric, ready to enjoy everything after the austerities and uneasiness of Eastern Europe, wanting to offer us mellow and beautiful sound; Klemperer, the old giant, really a nineteenth-century man, like Brahms himself, believing that man must face terrible things but will triumph in the end because he is brave and noble. There is much to be said against the nineteenth century, and now we have been saying it for a long time. But this was a century that knew how to make music.

3

After the Gala Opening, a Gala Champagne Party given by
the Junior League, which appeared to consist of a number of
pretty young women making their first and last appearance on
the Festival scene. The champagne they gave us was peculiar,
darkish and refusing to sparkle, as if dredged up far from
Rheims, but their eyes twinkled and their teeth shone. It was
a large party, the only one held in the Camelot Room of the
Daytona Plaza Hotel, and would have been more enjoyable if we
had not been plagued by photographers—the tyrants of this
age—who interrupted all promising talk, begged to be allowed
a moment, then spent ten minutes on each occasion pushing
us around, to make us look idiotic. Later parties—and there
were many of them—were given in private houses, and in
their food and drink, manners and style, seemed to follow a
set pattern. And while paying a tribute to the hospitality and
genuine kindness of these hostesses, I must confess I tried to
dodge the local guests, not out of any dislike of them but
because I wanted to talk to the musicians—conductors,
soloists, orchestral principals—when their long day's work was
done. They were very sedate, these parties, unless of course—a
shaming thought—they only really got going after our
departure; nobody was tight, plastered, stoned, nor even
boisterous; hosts and guests were on their best behaviour and
anyhow there was too much ice in everything. Sometimes, to
continue a talk quietly, one wandered out of the house to
stand in the garden or sit by the swimming pool, and then,
beyond air-conditioning, in the thickly pressing warmth of the
night, one was immediately bitten by mosquitoes. (They
feast on me at sight: it is Christmas at once to them when I
appear.) At the earlier parties, the local ladies generally put to
me one of two questions. The more knowing types—for this

[28

topic was high in the Festival buzz—asked me if we had our air-conditioning fixed now. The others, dimmer-sighted and dimmer-witted, wanted to know if I were Sir Arthur Bliss.

Master of the Queen's Musick, Honorary President of the L.S.O., and down on the Festival programme as one of the four 'guest conductors' and also 'composer in residence', and a friend of mine (I hope) for the past forty years, Sir Arthur had now arrived, after some delay, but had spent the first day or so fuming in his hotel room. I could sense his moustache bristling even on the telephone. And he was not angry without cause. Leaving Vancouver (which he had loved) to fly to Florida, he had been trapped in one of those sagas of wrong time-tables, delays, smogged-out airports, lost luggage. He had had to spend one night in an airport hotel, in a stuffy and hideous little room, with huge jets just clearing the roof every ten minutes. All this he described, with some new fire-and-brimstone touches he had not had time to think up on the telephone, when he came to lunch, obviously by then ready to enjoy—he is a great enjoyer, sizzling with gusto—Daytona Beach, the L.S.O. and the growing tale of misfortune. He has what every English composer needs—a large sense of humour. I delight in his taller and taller stories, and there is only one quirk of his that, if I did not allow for it, might mar our amiable companionship, which has even survived a colla-boration. He has never agreed to my discussing any musical subject with him, on the ground that he knows about music and I don't; but this has never prevented him from telling me about literature. There was an occasion, years ago, when, after suddenly discovering the novels of Henry Fielding, he insisted upon telling me about Fielding, without even giving me a chance to point out that I had written many thousands of words explaining and appreciating Fielding. However, I was glad to see my old friend and to sweat and to curse the climate together, and I looked forward to his march to the podium, almost turning the L.S.O. or the Institute Orchestra (of

29]

which, more later) into the band of the Grenadier Guards. All the same, I resented being mistaken for him, especially as several women said they recognized me as Sir Arthur from the photographs they had seen. 'My dear madam,' I cried to one of them, 'Sir Arthur Bliss has an enviable shock of white hair and a considerable moustache, and I have neither. You're just not *looking*.'

4

The Second Orchestral Concert brought us a new conductor, the prodigious André Previn, a dazzling array of musical talents and achievements, who attended the conservatories of Berlin and Paris, went to America in 1939 and was under contract to M.G.M. in Hollywood when he was sixteen, since which time he has attempted everything in music and succeeded everywhere. His manner and speech now at thirty-seven are entirely American, but somehow he looks more French than Charles de Gaulle. Just as the chubby-faced Kertesz conducts roundly and chubbily, so the pointed-faced Previn conducts pointedly, spreading out his feet and hunching up his shoulders, giving himself a triangular shape. Though he turns about a good deal, punching hard on his beat and his cues, one of the more experienced members of the orchestra told me that although he liked playing under Previn, he thought him rather too cautious, disinclined to let rip. Off the platform he is unaffected, quick and intelligent, very good company, and I liked him.

This concert began with Mozart's *Paris* symphony, and I for one took no joy in it. Not that it was played badly—all the notes were there, properly produced and timed, for after all this was a first-class orchestra—but it was played, so to speak, from the outside and not from the inside, where all the delicate fire is, and where Beecham and the old London Philharmonic always were when they played Mozart. It made me feel that as yet the L.S.O. isn't really *with* Mozart as it is with some nineteenth-century composers. The next work was de Falla's 'Love, the Magician', sung by Rosalind Elias, a charming Lebanese brunette always in danger of being overwhelmed by the orchestra. And I must confess that this spirited composition hasn't said very much to me for some time,

31]

though I understood what Previn meant when he told me later that he was fascinated by the economy of de Falla's orchestral effects. So to the long intermission, no drink but Coca-cola, and the orchestra drifting out of the stage door, mopping themselves, lighting cigarettes and, if they were gay young fiddlers, already keeping an eye out for the girls who somehow found themselves round there.

Then the concert came to life, with Prokofiev's Second Violin Concerto, written in 1935, one of his warmer works, a bottle of Sack, not Manzanilla. The soloist was our plane acquaintance, young Itzhak Perlman (he is only twenty-two but already has an American wife, equally young, very lively, not unlike a pretty monkey), who was born in Tel Aviv but studied at the Juilliard School of Music in New York. He is a young man of powerful build but has not the full use of his legs, so that he enters on crutches and has to play sitting down. This may make an audience feel more warmly towards him, but in fact to play long concertos without being able to stand, and on that crowded stage being hardly more prominent than all the accompanying violins, is to be gravely handicapped. Perlman triumphs—and with decent luck should succeed in more and more countries—because of the size and warmth of his playing. He belongs to the small group of *big* violinists, and after his performance of the Prokofiev, which was magnificent, he was awarded what the Americans like to call 'a standing ovation'.

This was no more than his due, and was not as rich a reward as it may first appear to be. Before I had done with the Peabody Auditorium I had joined, sometimes rather reluctantly, in a number of 'standing ovations'. What always happened was that after the applause had continued for a minute or two, a few people would stand up, others would follow their example, until most people were up on their feet. They were never general and spontaneous, rising like a great wave of joy and admiration and gratitude, something I have

[32

Daytona Beach.

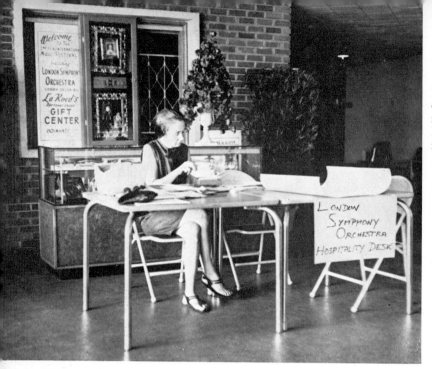

Mrs Carlson, one of the most active members of the Hospitality Committee.

Itzhak Perlman and J.B.P. arrive together.

The Orchestra, under Istvan Kertesz, giving a performance.

Istvan Kertesz conducting a rehearsal.

John Georgiadis (with one of his two sons), young leader of the Orchestra and of a group of dedicated young violinists.

Barry Tuckwell, principal horn and a master of that difficult instrument.

Roger Lord, principal oboe and a most sensitive musician.

Gervase de Peyer, principal clarinet and one of the renowned virtuosi.

William Bennett, principal flute and a fine soloist.

Stuart Knussen, principal double-bass— 'probably the best double-bass player in the world'.

Vladimir Ashkenazy rehearsing at the piano.

An international rehearsal with the Hungarian conductor (Istvan Kertesz), a Lebanese soprano (Rosalind Elias) and a Chinese bass (Yi-kwei Sze).

Szymon Goldberg talking to the heavy brass.

The heavy brass again, with Alan Jenkins on the tuba.

André Previn with the Perlmans.

known in London and in various European concert halls and opera houses. There was plenty of applause at the Daytona concerts, but not until the very last night did I ever sense any surge of feeling moving the whole audience. The clapping might go on and on and seem warmly appreciative and yet one felt, while making exceptions of many individuals of course, that behind it was a hollowness, a faintly chilly indifference, as if people were outside the essential experience, just tasting it; all of which, I feel, is peculiarly characteristic of American life in the urban and ex-urban middle-income brackets.

For the final item, every available man took every available chair and stand, for this was the suite from *Der Rosenkavalier*, which demanded—and got—the works. All the virtuosi seized their opportunities; Previn's head was almost lost between his shoulders and his arms got longer and longer; and towards the end, with the giant waltzes shaking the building, the steely L.S.O. strings sounded as if at any moment they might be white-hot. It was enormous and dazzling, of course, but even while I was applauding with the rest I couldn't help telling myself rather sourly that it didn't have to be so tremendous. After all, this wasn't the twilight of the gods or the dawn of doomsday but a little affair at the court of Maria Theresia. And what I took home—or rather to that night's party, to warm the over-iced bourbon—were certain moments of Prokofiev and Perlman.

5

Late next morning, having a corner of the Daytona Plaza bar, cool and dim as a cave, to ourselves, Bliss, now in splendid form though with some of his earlier indignation leaving its traces, held forth to me on conductors and conducting. He laid it down—with what might be called underfloor heating— that almost all orchestral players detest conductors who bring them in and encourage them with enormous gestures, prance and dance, mop and mow at them. I told him I had never collected opinions, though I had heard in my time ferocious criticisms of individual conductors, but I had often wondered about the players' reaction to this obtrusive guidance and encouragement. You are, let us say, leader of the 'cellos, sitting on the conductor's right. You and your men have to enter with great force, playing your heads off. And you can do no more, giving the maestro all you have. But there he is, turning to you, both arms sweeping up and down with the fingers curled towards you, as if demonstrating to the audience that all you have is still not enough for him, plainly suggesting that you and your boys could do more if you really tried and had at least some of his energy, enthusiasm, love of the work being played. This would seem to me, as they say, a bit much. And certainly the cunning old conductors never make this mistake. Not long before going to Daytona, I had stared down, from one of those Royal Festival Hall boxes high on the side, at Stokowski, taking the L.S.O. through a huge show-off programme; and he had controlled or commanded the most glittering or deafening effects using a few restrained gestures, an upraised finger here, a flicker of a hand there. In this way he seemed to announce that he, Stokowski, wasn't working hard, only the orchestra. Thus he was far removed from Bernstein, who at a previous concert, taking the L.S.O.

[34

through the fifth symphonies of Sibelius and Shostakovich, had worked himself into a frenzy and a lather, at times appearing to have both feet off the ground. But this is not mere exhibitionism—Bernstein no longer needs showmanship—but comes from his belief that a conductor must offer his audience a kind of visual image of the work in hand, a one-man ballet interpretation of it.

This leaves me unconvinced, and Bliss waved it away. Stick and hand should be almost thrown at the orchestra during rehearsal, not on the night. That was the method, he declared, of the old masters of the baton. To illustrate this, he described how he had attended some rehearsals by Nikisch— I think it was in Amsterdam just before the First War. (Earlier than that, incidentally, the first time I ever heard the L.S.O., it was being conducted by Nikisch.) The work in question was the overture to the *Meistersingers*, and at the first rehearsal Nikisch began by using huge emphatic gestures. At the second and third rehearsals—and there may even have been a fourth; I forget—the gestures were smaller and smaller, the orchestra knowing then what he wanted. And on the night of the performance, they were smaller still: there was a little pale-faced man, just bringing down a hand and crashing the audience into the solemn pageantry of mediaeval Nuremberg.

I will admit at once that the Third Orchestral Concert seemed to me to offer us an ill-arranged programme. It consisted of Mozart's Symphony No. 29 in A, his flute concerto No. 1 in G, then a concert version of Bartok's *Bluebeard's Castle*. I am against going from Mozart—and early Mozart, at that—to Bartok in one move. We need a halfway house provided by somebody—Berlioz perhaps. We had to jump from almost too much sweetness and light into blood, thunder, vinegar and tears. And Kertesz's Symphony No. 29 suffered from the same fault as Previn's *Paris* Symphony the previous night, which suggested to me that it was the orchestra itself that was to blame. They didn't play badly but it was as if they knew they hadn't yet got round to Mozart and were saving him up for real performances some time in the future. Their minds were brooding over the challenge and fury of Bartok, still to come, it seemed, and were content to jog through the Mozart symphony without, they hoped, appearing to be too dull. And they lost: they *were* dull.

The flute concerto was better all round, both in the solo part and its delicate accompaniment. The soloist was William Bennett, a handsome fresh-faced young man who ten years ago had even won a French government scholarship to study in Paris, which, if your instrument is the flute, takes a bit of doing. Bennett is the principal flautist of the L.S.O., taking the place of Geoffrey Gilbert, now a professor but over here again, in charge of the wind section at the Institute. (Have patience, we shall arrive at this Institute.) But in spite of Bennett's superb playing, I remain unconvinced that the flute is entirely satisfactory as a solo instrument, no matter what it can do—and how we should lament its absence—in the orchestra. For a solo instrument, set against all the others, it is to my mind *too innocent*. It is like a character in a novel or play who is all sweetness and goodness. The oboe and the clarinet are more rewarding in their solos because there is both good *and* evil in them, like Shakespeare's major characters.

The performance of Bartok's *Bluebeard's Castle* was very much an international occasion, revealing music to us in its U.N. aspect: a Lebanese soprano, a Chinese bass (Yi-Kwei Sze), a Hungarian conductor, a British orchestra, an American audience. I have never seen a stage performance of this Bartok opera—his only one, written in 1911—but have been told that its visual effects, with its seven doors opening one after the other, are very impressive. We could only stare at the two singers and the orchestra, and most of the time all that we heard was the orchestra, very fine indeed and clearly and powerfully directed by Kertesz. But the performance asked for more than two pleasant voices; it needed a pair of Wagnerian titans, to rise above the splendours and agonies of the orchestra, for which Bartok seemed to care more than he did for the human voice. But then Bartok is one of those original and formidable artists—and there are a number of these, belonging to various arts—whom I am ready to admire but don't really like. When I read the melancholy account of his final years of exile in America, I ought to have felt pity for him, but somehow I couldn't. Narrow, intense, fanatical, he isn't my kind of man; I keep my affection for broad, expansive, humorous and tolerant men, even though at this moment I may not be showing much tolerance myself. And in spite of the superb playing in the Bartok, I left this third concert feeling dissatisfied—partly with the programme, partly with myself, for I couldn't help wondering if the soggy climate, the afternoons I could neither keep awake nor sleep, the over-iced late-night parties, the inability to write and the lack of landscapes I wanted to paint, were combining to get me down. So while I was dragging myself to the typewriter to make a few notes, suggesting that the music wasn't good enough for me, it was possible that now I wasn't good enough for the music.

37]

7

At morning-rehearsal coffee breaks, then perhaps outside the stage door during the long intermissions, then again at these late-night parties (usually with few of the younger men there), I had a lot of easy talk with the musicians, cheerful chat and as yet no questions-and-answers, no probing on my part. I had decided even then that my final chapter here would be about orchestras in general and this one in particular, with as much knowledge and reasonable evidence as I could scrape together but without any names being mentioned. But no self-denying ordinances are necessary for this first week, so I don't propose to throw a blanket over certain figures or to pretend I have forgotten what came up in our talk together.

I remember, for example, one particular talk with Barry Tuckwell—Australian, handsome and thoughtful, Chairman of the Board of Directors of the L.S.O. and of course its principal horn player—and indeed, as we shall see, a marvel with that dangerous instrument. Unlike that other wonder-horn, poor Dennis Brain, he gives the impression of being strictly self-disciplined and also of being a very ambitious man, still youngish and not yet fully conscious of the drive of his ambition, but for all that—an agreeable companion. By arguing—really quite tentatively but with a show of dogmatism (I always sound more sure of everything than I really am)—that a symphonic orchestra, like an opera house, needs some ruthless boss man, I made him rise to the defence of orchestral self-government, which in fact is traditional with the L.S.O. from their original foundation in 1904. Part of Tuckwell's defence was that his fellow-performers, having to play alongside him, were the best judges of an instrumentalist, and that if he was playing slackly or was unreliable in other ways, they would know long before it was obvious to a conductor or general

[38

manager or dictator-impresario. But, I countered, wouldn't they tend to go easy with him just because he was, poor chap, one of the boys, in the same leaky boat, possibly with a sick wife or several difficult children? Not any more, I was told, or at least not in the L.S.O. A new breed of orchestral players had arrived. (And to this I hope to return, in the proper place.) Very well then, I went on, the orchestra voted into office its player-directors, who in turn, I assumed, would have to choose a permanent or at least principal conductor. Would they be likely to single out an autocratic trainer-conductor, a martinet devoted to long nagging rehearsals, a perfectionist like Szell if such a one happened to be available? Wouldn't they—perhaps quite unconsciously—move in the direction of a musician, reasonably well qualified, who happened to be good-natured, fairly easy-going, never too hard on the boys, who after all were the electorate? At which point, I seem to remember, we were interrupted by the hostess or some other lady.

A very different type, though coming from the same part of the world (and for some days I began to believe that all L.S.O. members came from Lancashire and Yorkshire or the Antipodes) was Alex Lindsay, a craggy-faced fellow, leader of the second violins and older than most of the string players. Let me say again here that the average age of the L.S.O. is about thirty-three, with most of the violins even younger than that; not excluding, I fancy, the concert-master himself, John Georgiadis, always amiable but apt to be a trifle uneasy, not very forthcoming, in my company, as if he didn't dislike me but couldn't help wondering—and I don't blame him—what the hell a writer was doing round there. Alex Lindsay was on his last stint—and a very demanding last stint too—with the L.S.O., for now he was halfway back to his native New Zealand, where he was under contract to lead—possibly to conduct—its symphony orchestra. A long sentence with the second violins, too often condemned to repeat the same notes while the first violins are off to fun and glory, can sour a man. Lindsay

39]

wasn't sour—and as an angler of amberjack, a hefty local fish, he could sound and look uproarious—but he was sharply critical of the musical London he had left behind. First, he thought it 'too commercial'. Secondly, he denounced its class-consciousness. I am usually ready to go with anybody along this line, but I was surprised—and remained somewhat sceptical—to be told that in our rehearsal rooms and recording studios, where most of us innocently imagine a classless society has been evolved, too much deference is paid to conductors who have been to public schools and ancient universities. Staring, no doubt rather goggle-eyed, at his craggily sardonic face—and wondering why the Antipodes so often show us this kind of face—I replied soothingly that class-consciousness was deeply embedded in us English, which indeed it is; but I also reminded myself that too many second-violin parts—*tumty-tum*, *tumty-tum*—might leave a man over-critical. However, I liked him.

Encountered on many occasions and always most warmly welcome, a man after my own heart, was Stuart Knussen, principal of the double-basses and a sort of genial viking from Manchester. 'He's probably the best double-bass player in the world,' I had been told, much earlier; and one of his juniors, promoted to sharing a stand with Knussen, declared: 'He's marvellous. Never knew anybody like him for under-standing all the music we're playing—he could put in the second horn part if he had to.' And certainly if I were a multi-millionaire and forming my own private orchestra, I would want Stuart Knussen even if he cost me as much as three ordinary double-basses. But this might suggest he's greedy, and he isn't, having turned down many American offers, to stay with the L.S.O. The mere sight of his gingerish head, up there beside the big fiddle, ought to make a conductor feel that all will be well in the music's cellarage. He was delighted to discover, in one chat we had, that I had long cherished a grievance against those English orchestras that made do with

[40

only six double-basses. This turned me into a man after *his* own heart, and led him to confide his belief that too many English conductors have been indifferent to a rich bass sound. We then shared a vision of more and more double-basses, and not condemned to be almost off the platform, where half their lion growls may be lost, but placed boldly in a row on top, as Koussevitsky (once a bass player himself) used to do and Stokowski still does. We had already discovered that we enjoyed the same kind of music, and now we furnished it with an ample and glorious bass—if only in a dream orchestra at midnight.

8

A brief return to an early theme—with a little development of it—to end this First Movement. On the Sunday the L.S.O. threw in a popular matinée, beginning with lighter Mozart and Schubert and then going on to the inevitable Strauss waltzes and polka, together with funny hats and a bit of clowning. Perhaps I ought to have gone, but I didn't, if only because I can do without all that Strauss, a July afternoon in Florida—and Sunday too—finds me in a sort of stupor, and I had already decided to go to the Auditorium that night to catch the repeat of the Brahms C Minor. And if I had gone, I would probably not have been sitting near Karen. But here she is, in a paragraph from the local paper:

> Bob Pope, of the International Speedway, took his family to hear the London Symphony's family matinée Sunday. Where some children her age would have wiggled just a little bit, his first grader, Karen, sat still, entranced, while the music filled the hall. Then, during one particular moving passage, she took her mother's hand and whispered, 'Mommie, are we still in Daytona Beach?'

So, to end this First Movement, we can set against all the Festival fund-raising and arrangements and fuss, the hundred men and their wives and children flown over the Atlantic in chartered jets, the two tons of baggage, the announcements and appeals, rehearsals and performances, just two small voices, that of the woman from out of town who said *I worked all year to come for these weeks*, and that of the little girl who asked *Are we still in Daytona Beach?* And suddenly the noise of calculating machines and typewriters, of roaring jets, clanking presses, angry or desperate committee members, instruments tuning up, the cries of programme sellers, can no longer be heard: the two voices have won; the movement ending, we might say, with one brief statement from a viola, then an oboe, thin, high and wondering.

[42

Second Movement

allegro moderato

T HIS Monday of the second week I remember as a crowded kind of day, complete with a nasty little accident. I had gone along, about the middle of the morning, to the Auditorium and there had found Bliss, a genial open-shirted brigadier, rehearsing his *Things To Come* film suite with the students' orchestra from the Institute. And these students— some of them professional musicians anyhow—were producing an unexpectedly good sound. They appeared to be of various ages and sizes, from poppets to stringy ladies, meagre adolescents to those young men who always seem larger and looser in America than anywhere else, so many badly finished giants. I decided to take a first look at the Institute while most of its students were busy here at the Auditorium, and as I didn't even know where it was, Herbert Cherin, general manager of the Festival, offered to take me along there. (At the opening concert, Cherin had insisted, politely but very firmly, upon taking away the camera of a young man sitting just in front of me, a demon who plainly intended not to listen to the orchestra but to 'shoot' it; and this prejudiced me in Cherin's favour.) The Institute was in fact only a few hundred yards away, and afterwards I always walked there from the Auditorium. As it was, when poor Cherin stopped his car outside the Institute, in an excess of politeness and zeal he jumped out to open my door for me, and in closing it he trapped my left hand, so agonisingly that for a moment I thought half its fingers had gone. No permanent damage was done—and I refused to see a doctor, not because I am brave but because I

43]

dislike the American Medical Association and its scale of fees —but it was damnably painful; and even now, as I write this, weeks and weeks afterwards and on another continent, two of my nails are partly deep blue instead of pink. And I mention this little accident because it left me with at least a stinging sensation for some days, and it may help to explain some of my grumpier judgments.

The Institute had taken over the large Junior High School, now in its summer vacation. (Some notices were still up: one said *Career of the Week*.) It was one of those buildings that have very long tiled corridors and are clean, hygienic and depressing. Going down one corridor after another, not hearing a sound from any of the classrooms, I began to feel like a character in some unpublished Kafka novel, in which a new young teacher would never find any pupils or even be able to report to the headmaster. However, on one of the upper floors I heard a piano and some singing, tracked them down and found they came from the opera group, rehearsing *La Boheme*. A young coloured girl, a slim and pretty soprano, was, I gathered, the group's notable discovery this year. On later occasions, when neither the L.S.O. nor the Institute orchestra was rehearsing, these corridors were filled with the sound of pianos, strings, woodwind, brass. This admirable enterprise was a joint venture of Daytona Festivals, Inc., and Stetson University, which supplied its admirable administrator, Dr Paul Langston. Most of its students were Floridans, but a few were already coming from other south-eastern states. And well they might too, with Ashkenazy taking master classes, Szymon Goldberg (we shall meet him soon) directing the String Programme and Geoffrey Gilbert the Wind, and L.S.O. principals giving advice to advanced students of their various instruments. What a chance! In this little section of Daytona Beach, in the few hundred yards that included the Auditorium and the Institute, now every summer there was being improvised—no, created—an academy of music of a very high standing. This was good, but still better—and I am following an old thought of mine—would have been a whole little town concentrating on music, a town in which your landlady could detect bad phrasing and the very bus drivers knew all about string quartets, the whole atmosphere of the place being saturated in music. The Americans and the Russians have done this for science and technology—then why not for music? The nurslings of such a town might prove to be a new and triumphant race of composers, conductors, instrumentalists.

After giving lunch to handsome Joan Chissell, here for *The Times* and being sensitive and intelligent for readers on each side of the Atlantic, we set out through a thunderstorm, with all roads awash, for a distant party given by a lively and ambitious hostess, Mrs Gorman, who was ready to entertain the whole L.S.O. and its wives. She liked such parties to have a theme, and this time it was the Wild West. We were promised something like a rodeo, on the beach below the end of her garden. The whole party should have been held in the garden but the downpour packed us indoors, where we wore comic Wild West hats, drank punch and ate fried chicken, and amused ourselves, so many gay cowboy sardines, as best we could. Bliss and I, egged on by photographers, wore our hats at strange angles, pointed pipes and pulled faces at each other; but my heart—together with aching left hand—wasn't in it; as an old Arizona man I had seen a number of real rodeos and didn't look forward to a Florida beach imitation of one. So I was thinking of stealthily taking my leave, even though the rain had stopped and it was possible now to go out into the garden. And I was soon thankful I hadn't left.

The early evening light was strange. It suggested some other place, without a name, and another time, not ours. No sunlight broke through the clouds still massed darkly above us, but between the edge of these clouds and the sea was a band of clear yellow light, so that everything down there on the beach could be distinctly, though strangely, seen. And then I saw

45]

what I had never seen before and can hardly hope ever to see again. Two thousand miles from the deserts where, years ago, I had watched such horses and their riders, now I looked down and saw young men in dazzling shirts and girls with flying hair riding in Western style, often at a gallop, along the very edge of the sea, appearing at times to be patterned in foam. For some minutes it was very clear and bright down there, in the strange yellow light above the sea. There are a few rare moments that seem to have an added dimension. They appear to return us briefly to scenes half-remembered from mythology. One of such moments was when I saw, breaking out of a wood near Alice Springs, a leaping golden line of kangaroos. And this scene of riders on the beach brought me another of these moments. Thank you again, Mrs Gorman, not for the comic hats and the punch (and the whisky you smuggled out to me from the kitchen) and the fried chicken, but for the enchanting frieze of horses and girls with flying hair against the sand and the foam.

We had some miles to go, driving slowly along roads still awash, and then had to take a shower and get into dry clothes, so when we reached the Auditorium for the First Chamber Concert, the first half of it was over. And I doubt if there were any more people there than we used to cram into our hall at Brook Hill, Isle of Wight, which meant that in this Auditorium there were about two persons for every row of seats. I have never wanted chamber music in large concert halls, and when such a hall looks almost empty my heart sinks. Even so, with my heart several fathoms down, I was able to feel sorry for the Iowa String Quartet, making their first appearance here, having been detached from their state university, just because their Beethoven (No. 9 in C) had to follow the Brahms trio, of which—more anon. The Iowa men, who play on a family of Strads lent them by a Washington museum, are well-trained and conscientious musicians, but they seemed too steady and clean-living for wicked old

Beethoven, who would probably be ordered off the campus at Iowa University. Besides, we had just heard the Brahms.

This trio for horn, violin and piano in E Flat was performed in that order by Barry Tuckwell, Perlman and Ashkenazy, who played as if they were no longer in this world but in another and better one, with no clay and iron in it, all delicate lights and shadows, brightening or fading colours, fashioned out of dream stuff. Any man believing Brahms to be thick and stuffy, the squarest of old squares, should be compelled to listen to this work, as performed by these three (they have agreed to record it), and then get down on his knees. Perlman and Ashkenazy couldn't have been better but it was Tuckwell's triumph—the horn being such a devil of an instrument to control—and especially in the middle movements, when his horn was so often mysteriously removed from us, calling us out of distant enchanted woods or castles already vanishing in the clouds. Is romance returning? I ask because this supremely romantic interpretation of the horn trio was the work, if it can be called work and not sorcery, of three musicians whose combined ages barely reach ninety. But I didn't leave the Auditorium wondering about the return of romance; I was furious because there had been so few people there. Also, my hand was still painful.

2

We passed several hours of the next day being entertained by a long-retired and indeed legendary Princeton professor. After lunch at the Country Club (not recommended) we crossed the Halifax river to his house, in what must be the oldest residential section of Daytona, a house so deep in vegetation and so darkened by it that we seemed to be in a tiny clearing in some forest. Eating superb cake and drinking champagne, real and cold, not Gala Night stuff, we lolled in the green dusk of his sitting room; and he and I talked about Santayana, whose pupil he had been—he was a Harvard man though he taught at Princeton—and I described how I had visited Santayana when his mind was wandering and he was being cared for by the Blue Sisters in Rome. Our host, approaching ninety, was older than Santayana had been, but he was spruce and alert, and he showed me among other things a device he had at his bedside for switching on a record-player. We thanked him and departed just as a thunderstorm came rolling and flashing, almost bringing midnight to this jungle-suburb. A few minutes later we were in a large store, buying a few things but taking our time because a cloud appeared to be bursting just above the street. So I was able to discover that one woman who served me was actually a Cockney, another had spent some time in London, and just round the corner was an Oxford student working here during his long vacation. Encounters of this sort, not infrequent, always bewilder me, making me feel I don't know enough. These people in the store had nothing to do with the visit of the L.S.O. to Daytona Beach, across the river. So what connection can there be between a store in Daytona, Florida, and London and Oxford? What determines these odd migrations? Are we being moved by demiurges playing chess with us?

[48

There were only three performers at that night's Chamber Concert—André Previn, a pianist as well as a conductor; Gervase de Peyer, the L.S.O.'s leading clarinet and a well-known soloist; and Szymon Goldberg, the violinist. De Peyer and Previn didn't appear to be very happy with the late Brahms Sonata in E Flat, rather as if they might have enjoyed playing Brahms separately but that together they might have preferred trying somebody else. And so it turned out, for they ended the concert with Poulenc's sonata, written for Benny Goodman in 1963, not long before Poulenc's death. This the boys, full of cheek, satire and jazz memories, like Poulenc himself, performed with superb technique and zest: it was music, good music too, we might say, in its impudent aspect. But between these two clarinet sonatas there had been Goldberg playing the difficult Debussy sonata of 1917; and earlier, up there all alone, Goldberg had shaped out of space, light and spirit, the Bach D minor Partita for unaccompanied violin.

Szymon Goldberg—and we saw much of him and his soft-voiced elderly wife—has had an extraordinary career. He was a child prodigy in his native Poland; at fourteen he played concertos with the Berlin Philharmonic; at sixteen he was concert-master of the Dresden Philharmonic; and at twenty he was concert-master under Furtwängler, back in Berlin. He left Germany in the later 1930s, was touring in Java when the Japanese arrived there and was interned by them for the following three years, during which his wife successfully contrived to hide his precious Strad. After the war he founded and conducted the Netherlands Chamber Orchestra, but has spent most of his time in America, though he is now, as I write, thinking of settling in London. He is a rather small and slight man, quiet and smiling, not—you would say— 'a personality'; yet when he appeared on that empty stage to play the Bach partita it was obvious at once that he was now in command of the Bach, his Strad, the stage, the audience, anything and everything within sight and hearing: little-man

49]

turned into giant diamond. And when he began to play, he was fifty not-so-little men who were still diamonds. I am as a rule too idle a listener, too fond of large dramatic effects and lush sound, to enjoy even the best unaccompanied violin solos; but for once I was entranced by this Bach partita, which flowed and cascaded, danced and glittered and sang, all out of Goldberg's fiddle and his imperturbable mastery, which could perform this partita, so huge and complicated, *much better than I can do anything*. But—and why shouldn't I be fair to myself?—I clapped as hard as anybody (bad hand and all), and if there was any scum of envy it was swept away by a rush of remembered delight and present thankfulness.

3

Wednesday morning's local paper brought an appeal from
the directors of the Festival that left me feeling exasperated, so
much so that I refused to record something in favour of it.
Innocent as an egg, it began as follows:

> Will Daytona Beach lose its Summer Music Festival because of a
> lack of attendance?
> Concerned by the financial picture facing us, we, the board
> members of the Festival, appeal earnestly to all who are interested in
> the Festival's continued success as the most important entertainment
> addition ever made to Daytona Beach's attractions.
> Our appeal today is simple—help save our Festival by coming to
> the concerts this week. The next few days are extremely critical ones,
> because of financial commitments that must be met. Full houses at
> Peabody Auditorium every night would help immensely. Buy a
> ticket today.

And then they added some stuff about its all being quite
comfortable and informal, no special clothes being necessary,
and so forth. A fine example of how not to do it. These well-
meaning directors were being honest but too naïve. After all, if
you can write about 'the most important entertainment
addition ever made to Daytona Beach's attractions', then you
are in show biz, Bach and Brahms notwithstanding, and so
might as well borrow managers' box-office tricks. An old show-
biz hand—especially an American one—would never appeal to
the public to fill the empty seats; he would never have admitted
he had any empty seats; he would have packed the hall—if
necessary 'papering' it—for the first few performances and
would have *turned people away*, knowing that most of these
people would then do their damnedest to get seats afterwards.
'New Yorkers,' said Cedric Hardwicke to me once, 'only want
to go to a theatre they can't get into.' And besides being poor
box-office tactics, appeals of this sort seem to me to humiliate

the musicians. Finally—though I will admit this is guesswork —I fancy this Festival should widen its whole appeal, declaring that it exists for the sake of all the south-eastern states, where they can't be all bankrupt or blockheads and some might like a week's holiday in or near Daytona, listening to magnificent music every night. But can't they hear music as good nearer home? No, sir or madam, they quite definitely can *not!*

I took these thoughts along with me to the Institute, where I found Geoffrey Gilbert, calm, easy, encouraging, in charge of a rehearsal of the full ensemble of the wind group. They were doing some Stravinsky in what seemed to be terrifying tempos. There must have been about forty of them altogether, with tender maidens playing flutes (very well too) in the front row and a number of those large and loose young men at the back blowing the brass. I was told that between 4.15 and 5.45 next day, all these wind players, together with the string groups, would be in master classes taken by the various L.S.O. principals; and news of this glorious opportunity should be determinedly spread, by those directors who drafted that dubious appeal, through all the states once in the Confederacy.

His rehearsal over, Geoffrey Gilbert, talking at ease, solved a riddle for me. But first I must add that Gilbert was seriously studying the flute at ten years of age, at twelve was playing in a cinema orchestra, entered the Manchester College of Music, where he is now a professor, at fourteen; and then, years later, after playing with the Hallé under Harty and with the London Philharmonic, in its great days, under Beecham, quietly but triumphantly revolutionized flute-playing in England. No longer had we to look to France for flautists: now we had our own. However, when he solved my riddle we were not talking about woodwind but strings. I couldn't understand what had happened to violinists. When I was younger, any amateur orchestra or scratch group of professionals was swamped with string players while it had to make do, more often than not, with less than a decent minimum of woodwind and perhaps brass, horns certainly. But now the strings—as Ministry of Food officials once liked to say—are 'in short supply'—that is, dam' scarce. This is true even of our leading symphony orchestras, including the L.S.O. itself. And Paul Langston, head of the Institute, told me that even the wealthy American orchestras are in the same plight. His point was proved by his own Institute Orchestra, so woefully short of first and second violins that for its public performance (and we shall come to it) some youngsters from the back desks of the L.S.O. had to be smuggled in to give it a reasonable string tone. So where have the fiddlers gone? Geoffrey Gilbert's reply was that we are now short of violinists because our Higher Education, demanding passes on various levels, takes youngsters away from their fiddles—say, at fifteen—just when they need to keep in constant practice, if they are to be professional violinists. What is lost during these middle teens is very difficult to restore later. So what we gain on the roundabouts, we lose on the strings.

Dutifully I attended the concert given by the Institute Orchestra: Brahms's Third Symphony, conducted by Robert Hause, a tall young man—perhaps the tallest—from Stetson University; Bliss taking his *Things To Come* suite; André Previn conducting Britten's *Young Person's Guide to the Orchestra*, in which Jacquetta takes a maternal interest because she helped to bring it into existence—in its original form as a film project—when she was responsible for Visual Education at the Ministry, just after the war. I went up into the balcony for this concert, and from there the extraordinary composition of this orchestra was quite plain—for example, it had only five double-basses but twelve 'cellos, and actually more trombones than it had violas. In these circumstances, though the students made a gallant effort, both the Brahms and the Britten were too searching and not very rewarding. I thought Bliss came off best—and incidentally revived memories of my friends H. G. Wells and Alex Korda in the 1930s—but as Bliss refuses to allow me to talk about music, he will certainly not want me to write about his—so I will stop here.

4

I am now staring at my notes—and not hopefully—for this is all they tell me: *Interlude here—possibly painting on beach—and beach life generally*. Going upstairs to the boy's room, pecking those ten words out on my typewriter there, probably seemed a good half-day's work in Crescent Ridge Road, Daytona Beach; but now in Alveston, Warwickshire, and a temperate climate, feeling conscientious and energetic, I curse that idle fellow and his *Interlude here*, and his *possibly painting on beach* and even worse, a despicable fobbing off, his *beach life generally*. If he couldn't find anything to add to his miserable *beach life generally*, how in the name of Heaven could he expect me, now three thousand miles away, to fill it in for him? (This is not my usual attitude towards my notes, which almost always seem ineffectual and rather touchingly pathetic, like so many favourite characters in Russian fiction and drama.) Well, I don't propose to say anything about beach life, which has the same mindless routine the world over, except that in Daytona, on bright mornings, the dry sand, out of the tide's reach, glared so fiercely that I could only look at it unwateringly through dark glasses. And I can't paint wearing dark glasses. (Can anybody? Or is there a successful Dark-glasses Group now?) So it was probably during this mysterious *Interlude* that Jacquetta, tired of seeing me with my face streaked in sweat and my eyes watering, weary too of trying to persuade me to hire a cabaña so that I could paint in its shade, firmly commanded a man to bring one, coloured like a tiger, and installed me under it. (In our strictly domestic politics, she represents the progressive and experimental party while I am deeply sunk into an obdurate conservatism—I had never hired a cabaña and didn't propose to hire one now, that kind of thing.) I did several beach sketches, in or out of cabañas, and

55]

enjoyed trying to capture the dimming vistas of dunes and motels on one side and of the waves curling and creaming, with a few bright little figures, on the other side. But at some sacrifice of realism I obliterated all motorcars, reversing time to about 1907, happily wiping out sixty years with the cars.

The Fourth Orchestral Concert, conducted by Previn, appeared to me to have drawn the largest audience we had seen so far, probably about four-fifths capacity. There was a good reason for this, but I will disclose it later. Two works in Previn's programme were quite new to me. The first was Bernstein's *Overture to Candide*, that ill-fated musical. But whatever went wrong with it, certainly it began well with this overture, brief and lively, crisp as a new digestive biscuit; and on a first hearing I preferred it to anything else I had heard of Bernstein's. The other work new to me had been first performed in the year of my birth, 1894, a fact to which I cannot attach any significance whatever. This was Symphony No. 1 in G Minor by Carl Nielsen, the Danish composer, whose work appears to be now struggling towards some general recognition. Though it did seem to get better as it went along, I must confess that I listened to it rather sleepily. It tended to sound like some noble nineteenth-century symphony that had suffered an accident and had been left under water too long. The third item was anything but new to me, an old favourite, Stravinsky's *Firebird* suite, which I had heard the L.S.O. play, not long before, under Stokowski, doing all manner of wonderful glittering tricks with it. Previn is no old maestro yet, and the Peabody Auditorium is not the Royal Festival Hall, but he and the enthusiastic L.S.O. virtuosi did contrive to suggest aurally those long-vanished juggling acts that lit up the stage with curving and gleaming Indian clubs. A fine dazzling performance.

However, I have kept to the last the work that was un-doubtedly responsible for the larger audience: Tschaikowsky's Violin Concerto, with Perlman as soloist. 'It stinks in the ear',

[56

wrote Eduard Hanslick—I am borrowing this from a programme note—who was then the most influential music critic in Europe. And poor Tschaikowsky, whatever he might be offering, has been stinking in the ear of most music critics ever since. They can be excused their impatience and scorn; they hear him far too often, taking the place too of composers they want to hear. But if they can be excused, then they in turn should be easier with the public. After all, Tschaikowsky's continuing popularity is not hard to understand. He is unusually tuneful; he is extremely skilful; and what he is trying to express is what nine people out of ten want music to express, from a honeymoon sweetness to all manner of tantrums. He represents their idea of a musician. It is only the tenth listener who is anxious to share Bruckner's love of God or Mahler's deeply introverted revelations of himself. The violin concertos of Beethoven and Brahms, to be heard on future programmes here, may be—and indeed are—nobler works than Tschaikowsky's, but any fiddler telling the truth will admit that his is a thundering good concerto. So if you want a violin concerto—and there are times when I don't— then why not accept the Tschaikowsky again? Perlman, who gave us a magnificent performance of it and who is, I would say, a young man incapable of affectation and deceit, told me later that night he loves it. And, after all, he must have spent more hours with it than any critic.

Finding myself with Ashkenazy, going out of the hall, which empties slowly, I told him that there was to me more essential *Russianness* in the mysterious bass opening of the *Firebird* than in all the Tschaikowsky. He agreed about that opening, which creates at once the semi-oriental atmosphere of fairy-tale Russia, but maintained that Tschaikowsky was equally Russian too in his own way. And he should know! Perhaps we remember too often the Russia of the steppes fading into the Urals and Asia, and forget—if we don't happen to be reading one of the great old novels—the Russia of the country houses and the Petersburg *salons*, which Tschaikowsky understood so well when he was composing the score of *Eugene Onegin*. Incidentally, Ashkenazy excused himself from a small supper party that had been arranged; he wanted to go home—and it was now after eleven—to do *four hours' practice!* I thought of myself shuffling up to the typewriter, grumbling as well, to set down about a hundred words of notes, and wondered if I was a lazy old fraud. Still—I wasn't on my way towards another 'standing ovation'.

The little supper party took us to a large and darkish restaurant, serving not-very-Italian Italian food, and staffed by large and darkish waitresses, impatiently patient like teachers who had been too long with a class of mental defectives. Present were the Perlmans, Previn and his friend Schuyler Chapin from Lincoln Center, Barry Tuckwell, ourselves. The musicians, just like actors, talked gossipy shop spiced by humorous anecdotes, the kind of conversational stuff you either enjoy, as I do, or equally detest, as Jacquetta does. However, I halted its flow by declaring with mock solemnity that the heat and humidity were making me feel less and less susceptible to the charms of music. There were moments now, I told them, when I began wondering if I really liked listening to it. They didn't believe me and I didn't want them to, yet in fact it wasn't all nonsense. A grain of truth was somewhere there. It was not only that the climate did make music seem less important, just as it made almost everything else seem less important; on a deeper level, well beyond conscious control, old associations were protesting against symphonies and concertos that followed a glaring morning and an afternoon thunderstorm and then arrived in evenings like baths of warm milk. In London and New York, Vienna and Moscow, I had gone in and out of symphony concerts in the peculiar chilled-smoke atmosphere of late autumn or the snow and iron of winter. And these associations went back and back to my first concert-going, as a lad in

[58

Bradford, some years before World War One when we would wait outside the door of the West Gallery in St George's Hall, on bitter evenings, to climb half-numbed a thousand stone steps—to listen to the Hallé conducted by Hans Richter or to hear Kreisler, Casals and Bauer play the Schubert Trio in B flat. And then afterwards there was warmth in the heart to defy the sleet outside. (Remember—no turning music on and off like a tap! When we youngsters at last heard the *Eroica*, we had gone some way towards earning it.) So, I repeat, though what I said was meant to tease the musicians, it wasn't complete nonsense; the grain of truth was there: deep down I am an autumn-and-winter lover of music.

On the afternoon before the Fifth Orchestral Concert, we went to Tomoka State Park, where I hoped I would find something I would want to paint. This park, only a few miles inland from Daytona, is officially declared to be beautiful; and, without wishing to be offensive, I must say that this precious term, *beautiful*, is much too loosely used in Florida. Tomoka State Park is not beautiful. Fishermen and children can spend a pleasant afternoon there, but the park itself seemed to me less attractive than the road that took us there, which did at least offer us glimpses of various kinds of herons and egrets and was often deep in the shadow of live oaks immensely curtained by Spanish Moss, as if giant spiders had once woven webs there. I am sorry if this sounds too sinister for an innocent plant, which is not even a parasite and can hang on anything, even wires, simply to take moisture out of the air; but I have never been in the Deep South and seen the live oaks so thickly festooned with Spanish Moss without feeling I was about to enter one of the darker novels of William Faulkner, that incest and murder were close at hand, that in some plantation house hidden behind these greenish-grey-beard curtains were corruptions and abominations. And I offer no defence of this feeling.

Bang in the middle of the park is a group of statuary that you may regard with wonder and admiration:

> Visitors can admire the massive, startlingly-coloured group of statuary, depicting the Indian legend of *Tomoki*, a Timicuan chieftain, designed and executed by the internationally known artist and sculptor, Fred Dana Marsh. . . .

And again, without wanting to be offensive, just telling the plain truth, I must declare that this large statuary group may have successful rivals in places I have never visited but that it

remains in my memory the ugliest I have ever seen anywhere
—bad taste's most striking monument. Hurrying away from
it, I decided to paint a possible little subject—live oaks and
palms dark in the foreground with glimpses between them of
water and a bright sandbank. So I spread out my gear and
settled down, though the inevitable thunderstorm was rolling
round not far away and the sky was preparing itself for a
gigantic production of *Macbeth*. But not only was the light
thickening as I set to work, I was soon being savagely bitten.
This was unendurable, and I packed up, with an unfinished
sketch that never deserved to be finished. This defeat, following
the disappointment of the park itself, and with the bites now
at work on me, made me feel cross, and I suspect I must have
stayed cross all the evening. And this possibly explains why I
found this Fifth Orchestral Concert so unrewarding—I just
didn't want to *be* rewarded.

Bliss conducted, and did it very well in his rather military
no-nonsense style. I have no complaint against him either as
conductor or composer. (The programme included, as a final
item, his own Colour Symphony, first performed—and by the
L.S.O.—forty-five years ago. But, once again, I will accept his
ban, and keep silent.) An earlier item was Mozart's Clarinet
Concerto in A, K.622. This is a ravishing work but Gervase
de Peyer left me unravished. He is of course a brilliant
performer, one of the L.S.O.'s star virtuosi, but—and of course
this may have been because I was not in a good temper—he
made me feel—as indeed the orchestra did too—that he didn't
really want to be playing Mozart, like a man ill-at-ease wearing
powdered hair and satin knee-breeches. Coming immediately
before Bliss's Colour Symphony was Handel's Concerto for the
Harp in B Flat, played by the L.S.O.'s principal harpist, Osian
Ellis, who ought to look like a Welsh bard but doesn't. It is a
cheerful, small-scale work, to which Ellis added some ex-
quisite filigree. However, it was none of these but the first item
on the programme that reinforced my crossness.

61]

The work in question was Elgar's *Cockaigne* overture, and there was nothing wrong with the performance of it. So what was wrong with me? Simply this—that I wanted more and better Elgar. I have yet to meet an American concert-goer who really knew anything worth knowing about Elgar. Most Americans I have met—though a few of them might have heard the *Enigma* variations—appeared to associate Elgar with one or two Palm Court pieces and pompous Edwardian marches. They had never heard *Falstaff*, the *Introduction and Allegro*, the *Cello Concerto*, the two symphonies—to name my own favourites. I realize the difficulty of programme-planning for a season of this kind, which will inevitably have to accept works reasonably familiar to the orchestra, time for rehearsal being so limited; and no conductor in his right mind is going to offer an audience *Falstaff* after spending only a morning on it. But then I feel that *Falstaff* should have been in the repertoire anyhow, ready for Daytona or anywhere else. Elgar's fat knight isn't mine—and I have broadcast for an hour and published a long essay on Falstaff—and Elgar's tone poem cannot help celebrating the steely triumph of Prince Hal. This was inevitable because he was working against the grain of his musical personality, which could easily suggest magnificence and nobility, a deep melancholy, an aching wistfulness, but came with difficulty to wit and humour. Strauss, the extravert, could have given us a good rough-and-tumble, sack-and-bawdy Falstaff, though perhaps rather more of a beer-garden roisterer, a bawling German comic, than we should like to accept; whereas the introverted Elgar—and he was a pro-foundly introverted type, even though by the time I met him he was pretending to be a retired colonel off-to-the-races—could have looked deeper into Don Quixote than Strauss did. And in spite of all its literary and psychological limitations, his *Falstaff* is a glorious piece of music—and of course very English, like all Elgar's major work. And why wasn't at least one example of this major work being brought to the

[62

Americans? We don't all have to agree with those Central European conductors who ignore Elgar. (I once asked Bruno Walter why he never played Elgar and he said he found the music not sufficiently concentrated. So I stared at him— nicely, I hope—and said 'Bruckner'?) And later that night, grumpy at a party, I complained of this L.S.O. neglect of Elgar to one of its members, who told me that it was generally believed in his circle that the L.S.O. directors had 'a thing' against Elgar. To which I replied that they ought to be ashamed of themselves. But of course I was in a bad mood.

6

This Saturday was 'Festival State Day', which must have meant something because it brought a crowd of us, musical or political or busybodies like me, to an unusually good dinner at the Daytona Plaza Hotel. (It seems ridiculous, a challenge to all sound sense and tradition, that an Englishman should find himself being handed not only bigger but better slices of roast beef in Florida than he discovers anywhere now in England.) But though the food was excellent and the whole scene quite impressive, I was haunted by a fear—and it tempted me to gobble—that very soon some of the politicians present, with a pound of red beef inside them, would begin to make speeches at us. (It was said of one American politician that whenever he saw half a grapefruit he began at once 'Mr Chairman, Ladies and Gentlemen, Friends—') And perhaps I am looking back at this 'Festival State Day' dinner through a golden haze, just because either the politicians unaccountably decided not to make speeches or somebody, perhaps packing a rod, told them to shut up or else. To finish one's dinner and talk at ease, without being hammered at and silenced and compelled to listen to droning windbags, was wonderful. I have had to make a lot of speeches, all kinds, in my time, and if I am considered an able performer, this is partly because I can be heard easily but chiefly because—and this is particularly important with after-dinner speeches—I am always *shorter* than people expect me to be. This frees them from keeping quiet and listening, so in their relief they say they could have done with more from me. Asked if I like making speeches, I always reply quite truthfully that I don't but that what I dislike even more is listening to other men's speeches. What I enjoy are good food and drink and chat and no speeches: the 'Festival State Day' dinner at the Daytona Plaza Hotel.

[64

Humming with protein, off we went to the Auditorium, which appeared for once to be sold right out. Saturday night and the State Day may have helped but it was really Perlman and Previn who drew most of the crowd. Previn was of course conducting the orchestra—and I thought that on this occasion he did uncommonly well—and Perlman played the Brahms Concerto. It was an extraordinary performance for a violinist still in his early twenties, far more remarkable than the Tschaikowsky, for Brahms never wrote any of his major works for musicians in their early twenties—he was, we might say, a middle-aged man writing for middle-aged men. Perlman was at once clear and warm, thoughtful and impassioned. I can see him now, many weeks afterwards, swaying in his chair—for, remember, he can't stand up to play—his broad heavy face shadowed and then turning up to the light. I am proud to have shared a plane, a photograph and a lot of pasta with this astonishingly accomplished young man. And I must add that Previn and the L.S.O. really did an accompanying job for this Brahms, on a level that had not been reached before. The audience loved them all.

Brahms's friend, Joachim, lent him some of his own fiddle expertise for this concerto. And I was thinking during the intermission, when the foyer was so crowded I fought my way to the huge warm night outside, how at the time they were written these famous violin works were considered too difficult for anybody except a great virtuoso even to attempt; whereas now, hundreds of advanced students in conservatories all over the world do not hesitate to learn them, at least playing all the notes. We have bounded forward in technique, though not in creative splendour. I was also remembering how an elderly Manchester man, whose parents used to have Joachim staying with them when he was giving a concert in that city, told me that the great violinist was always so nervous and apprehensive that he himself, only a boy then, felt quite disturbed. But perhaps Joachim had a special fear of English audiences,

65]

regarded with suspicion then by most visiting maestros. It has been said that von Bülow so disliked this *land ohne musik* that he deliberately played wrong notes for some English audiences. (*One wants but little Herr Bülow, Nor wants that little long.*) Yet our Royal Philharmonic Society rescued Beethoven when Vienna could do no more for him, and substantially helped more than one European composer afterwards. And now London has four symphony orchestras—five, if one includes the B.B.C.—and listens to more music than any other capital city. So over such thoughts I smoked my pipe, which never tasted better than it did outdoors during one of these intermissions, not knocking it out until I was summoned back to my seat.

The whole of the second half was claimed by Rachmaninoff's Second Symphony in E Minor, a work that had been completely unknown to me—though I enjoy Rachmaninoff—until quite recently, though now I know it fairly well through recordings. It is too long for what it has to say, demanding some fifty minutes even with cuts, and it has some passages that could not have suggested film music in 1907, from which it dates, but do so now—though film music on a high level. On the other hand, it owes less to Tschaikowsky, I think, than some music critics would have us believe, for Rachmaninoff has his own voice and style; and it seems to me fascinatingly expressive of 1900–1914 Russia, with its sudden highlights and deep shadows, the Russia of Andreyev and the earlier Blok and the half-hysterical pessimism, against which Soviet authority, demanding socialist arts and a brassy optimism, set its grim face. And while great creations rise above their age, there is always, I fancy, a validity about work that completely expresses its own period. (And if you ask me why Rachmaninoff as a symphonist is coming into fashion again, I could find you a reply, but prefer to pass on.) It cannot have been many years after he wrote this symphony that I saw and heard Rachmaninoff, then giving recitals in the

[66

North of England, where his Prelude in C Sharp Minor was being thumped out on hundreds of pianos. (I played it myself, after a fashion.) I recollect his appearance better than I do the exact quality of his piano-playing, perhaps because he offered such a sharp contrast to most of the other star soloists of that time. They were usually shaggy-haired and massive, whereas Rachmaninoff was closely cropped, thin, with a rather indeterminate, perhaps reluctant, presence. He refused to radiate self-confidence, to bask in the lights and applause, like most of the others. Both in his playing and in his compositions, behind the assured technique there is something shadowy and melancholy, as if he had known, years before 1917, that he would end as an exile.

Previn had recorded this Second Symphony with the L.S.O., and though he was still careful, perhaps too careful, to bring everybody in, it was clear at once that every damp white shirt up there contained a man who knew exactly what he had to play and how he should play it. So Previn in his hunched-up pointed fashion went to town. He was able to display to us with wonderful effect those particular L.S.O. qualities, the elegance and the zest and the fire, which he mentions whenever he declares, on both sides of the Atlantic too, that this is his favourite orchestra. So we had, for example, the superb elegance of Gervase de Peyer's clarinet in the *Adagio* and the overwhelming attack of the young strings, now almost steaming, in the last few minutes of the finale. I don't know how many ruined bow ties rose to face our 'standing ovation', but their wearers certainly earned one.

After this concert I missed a trick, for which I apologize to livelier readers. We had accepted an invitation to a party being given by two of the most robust and gregarious characters in the L.S.O., northcountrymen too—the piratically bearded-and-shirted Frank Mathison, ready to walk straight on in *Peter Pan* as well as play his noble bass trombone, and the broad-faced euphoric Alan Jenkins, who combines the orchestra's tuba with its treasury. There was something vaguely nautical about this party, for under Mathison's command the L.S.O. competes in a sailing race against local enthusiasts, but what was certain about it was that it would go on more than half the night and be fairly uproarious. And after that dinner and that concert and with eleven o'clock come and gone, we knew we just couldn't take it, and so begged off, going to bed for once before midnight. I seem to remember taking another look at Marshall McLuhan's *Understanding Media*. 'The most important thinker since Newton, Darwin, Freud, Einstein and Pavlov', the *New York Herald Tribune* is quoted as saying—and it must have been its death-rattle. For over fifty years I have been indulging in wild generalizations to keep talk going, but compared with what McLuhan can set down in print, anything I have ever said might have come from a cautious physicist being interviewed by *Nature* or *Mind*. I took a few pages, watching a few sketchy little original ideas being blown up into vast hot-air balloons, and then went back to a detective story. Early night nothing! It must have been well after two when I got to sleep, and not, I think, because I am so sensitive to Brahms and Rachmaninoff: it was all that State Day beef.

7

On this Sunday, July 23rd, I never heard a note of music. (There was a repeat at night of the Fourth Orchestral Concert, but there was nothing I wanted to hear again so soon.) Coming down rather late for breakfast, probably half-witted, all I saw in front of me was a pleasant idle day, whereas in fact I was kept hurrying from one engagement to the next like a crazy debutante. The first thing I had forgotten was that I had promised to give an interview that morning to Michael Steinberg, for the Boston *Globe*, which had sent him to the Festival because he is its music critic. He had also taught music at various colleges. We had run into each other several times at the concerts. He was—and, I hope, still is—a youngish German-American, amiable as well as intelligent though perhaps a trifle over-solemn. I forget how the interview went, what questions he asked, how I replied to them, but when we stopped that nonsense and talked like men and brothers, I remember his telling me that he admired the L.S.O. strings— very fine indeed, keener and more forceful than American string-players. But when I went on to boast about our English woodwind, the triumphant creation of masters like Leon Goossens, Frederick Thurston, Geoffrey Gilbert, though he admitted our woodwind was remarkable (and this could have been mere politeness), he warned me that most American conductors, woodwind players, and possibly critics, would not agree to this. They were all highly critical of English woodwind sound, finding it too open, vibratory, aggressive.

I didn't tell the polite Steinberg that if they didn't like it, they could lump it. That would have been altogether too open, vibratory, aggressive. But I told myself, after he had gone, that the great and rich American orchestras and their admirers had perhaps been too long under the spell of Central European sound, a tradition arriving by way of Vienna and *gemütlichkeit*. To achieve this mellow tone, soothing the wealthier patrons, the woodwind—especially the clarinets and oboes—had to produce what has been called a 'dark' sound, removed and mysterious, which undoubtedly demanded exceptional technical resources. Indeed, discussing this with me later, one of the L.S.O. directors, himself a woodwind player, said, 'The best of them have probably got a better technique than we have. But they lack musical imagination.' And certainly our great teachers, who had created this new school of English woodwind-playing (and I had known some of them·and had heard them play in private as well as in concert halls) had had this musical imagination. An obvious example was Leon Goossens, who, by sheer individual artistry, had plucked the oboe out of the orchestra and transformed it into a solo instrument.

Just as he was leaving, Michael Steinberg reminded me that we should be meeting again shortly, that very afternoon on the platform of the Peabody Auditorium. He and Bliss and I were to perform there as a *Panel*, to answer questions from the audience that the chairman, Paul Langston, would read out to us. I had in fact never been asked if I wanted to take part in this organized imbecility, and if I had have been asked I would have replied, as I had done scores and scores of times before, right from the beginning of the B.B.C.'s Brains Trust, both on radio and television, *Certainly not*. But somehow I had been publicly committed to this gruesome caper, so I went along. It was a bad idea from every point of view. Thus, the time was wrong, because very few people want to sit in a hall at 2.30 on Sunday on a summer afternoon. Most people are either out for the day or upstairs at home almost in a state of coma. Again, the last place for a small audience questioning a *Panel* is a huge auditorium, where the three wise men have to stare at rows and rows and rows of empty seats. However, I must add that our audience may have lacked quantity—and I

[70

doubt if there were a hundred in all—but had quality. The questions were sensible and our answers, even if not always equally sensible, were enjoyed.

There was only one question I remembered clearly. Was a technical knowledge of music necessary in order to appreciate it? Bliss charged in at once, as if in command of the Light Brigade. Of course it was necessary, otherwise you merely wallowed in sound like his friend Mr Priestley (*laughter*). His friend Mr Priestley replied at once that he loved wallowing in sound (*laughter*), though he had some elementary knowledge of music. (So I have, too.) He also pointed out that while he could if need be talk for days on the technique of writing, directing and acting plays, he thought that audiences could enjoy them without the benefit of such technical instruction. What Bliss said to this and what I retorted, I have forgotten, but I think we kept our caps-and-bells jingling, banged each other over the head with verbal bladders, for a few more minutes. There was to my mind an interesting sequel to this lively exchange, almost two weeks later, when Bliss had long been back in St John's Wood. I was at a dinner party and the woman sitting opposite to me, apparently a very conventional type, had been asserting her belief in conformity to her two neighbours. But then she looked across at me, and said, 'But I must tell you, I was at that *Panel* and what struck me—and I admired it—was the way in which you and Sir Arthur Bliss seemed to be completely yourselves, just saying what you wanted to say and not caring what people thought about you.' I told her that we were two elderly self-employed professional men, and so we didn't give a damn; and I was then left wondering how she squared her remarks to me with her belief in conformity, wondering too if many American women drove their husbands and sons to conform and then secretly despised them because they couldn't say they didn't give a damn.

If at this point I begin to write like the social columnist of the *Daytona Beach Evening News*, who calls herself *Chatterbox* and must lead the life of a whip-top during the Festival, this is because I have been reading cuttings from her column, provided by our secretary who, it must be remembered, was very much on the spot. Without *Chatterbox*, pointing and clapping hands and almost screaming, some of these social events would be a mere blur. But there are also significant little items to be found in her column, as, for example: 'Carolyn and George Wendell drove 500 miles—from their place in Bluffton, S.C.—to attend Saturday night's L.S.O. concert.' We like our L.S.O. concerts in London, but few of us would drive from Aberdeen to attend one. And this is the way the Festival should go, drawing on the whole south-east of the U.S. My own notes for this late Sunday afternoon are terse: *After Panel went out to party arranged for J. and me—given by sympathetic art dealer and very pleasant wife—some writers, few musicians—good party, not too crowded—excellent food and drink —back home about 7.30.* But *Chatterbox* fills me in with her account of 'visiting literati . . . gathered in Henry's high-ceilinged studio, its walls lined with books and paintings. . . .' and much else, including a little episode, which has fled my memory, that has me autographing a copy of *It's An Old Country* for *Chatterbox*:

> I was rather diffident about asking Mr Priestley to autograph it, but I had orders from mother and an assist from Winch. I told him my mother wanted him to inscribe the book and I think he actually twinkled as he replied: 'I always autograph books for people's mothers or people's children but never for people.'

That 'I think he actually twinkled' suggests now that the Daytona photographs did not distort my appearance, that I really was looking like something between Goering and a quack doctor while I was there, surprising *Chatterbox* by what might actually have been a twinkle. But I do remember some talk with a few other members of 'the literati'—and some who had accepted invitations never turned up, a dirty trick many writers in many countries are always playing—and I have

[72

some recollection now of talking to Barry Tuckwell in the garden, where we had gone to cool off, and of starting to question him about his attitude towards his native Australia— about which I was sharply curious—but then of course we were interrupted.

Nor was the day done with us. After dining at home, we were called for at about 10.30 to be taken to a late-night party, going early because I was fulfilling a promise to our hostess, Mrs Huysman, to give her an interview for various Florida papers and, I think, the *Chicago Tribune*. After the routine questions and answers, we wondered together how the whole base of this Festival could be broadened, Mrs Huysman proving herself to be as sensible as she was vivacious and tenacious. Then, the concert over, the musicians joined us, and I was able to have a final and warming exchange with Previn and Perlman, who were leaving Daytona next morning. The party thickened and heated up. Jacquetta and I slipped out to sit on a balcony, and it was really beautiful (no Tomoka State Park nonsense now) out there, overlooking a moonlit sea that had one long silver wave. Out there too was one brooding Celtic harpist, Osian Ellis, who, after he had talked, like a good Welshman, about local religious life, answered some questions I put to him—but slowly and easily, not to disturb the moonlight and that solitary bright wave down there—questions about the orchestra and its organization that have no place here. We went home about 1.30, one of us full of food and drink he didn't really want and shouldn't have had. It had been a long day and the best thing in it had been the sight of that lonely wave curling in the moonlight.

Third Movement

poco allegretto

W<small>E</small> were pleasantly committed, at the beginning of this third week, to the Volusia County Historical Commission, which would take us, along with others, to some plantation ruins not too far away (Daytona is in Volusia County) and then sustain us with some refreshment. Jacquetta and I were picked up by a determined elderly lady, well-informed and intelligent but formidably loquacious, who sprayed us with facts and fancies as she somehow conveyed us through the Daytona traffic and then into a wilderness. A hundred and fifty years ago, before this tangle grew, all these had been well-cultivated plantation grounds. We were asked to admire—and did indeed admire—a wonderful old live oak, probably over a thousand years old, that had branches as thick as the trunks of other trees, many of them disappearing into the ground, as if this monster live oak were turning itself into a banyan tree. In a clearing in this wilderness was all that was left to be seen and wondered at of what once had been called Bulowville, a very prosperous plantation—the wealthiest of all the plantations along the Halifax River—owned by the Bulow family. It was nothing more than the ruin of a sugar mill, but, like so many earlier industrial buildings, massively constructed, it had a certain dignity of its own, so that these blackened walls, seen against a background of what might almost have been Amazonian jungle, were oddly impressive.

When young John Joachim Bulow, a handsome and high-spirited youth, inherited this plantation, his immediate prospects were bright, his future enviable. Behind these walls

[74

of coquina rock, the gigantic iron rollers unceasingly crushed the sugar cane, cut and gathered by those slaves, of the many hundreds there, who were not working in the cotton fields, building new plantation houses, or helping to load the schooners and flat-boats on the Halifax river. And not only was Bulowville prosperous, it was also largely self-supporting. Afterwards there were legends of young John Joachim's wild doings—and some Florida storytellers made the most of them —but all historical evidence suggests that he knew how to run his estate and was in fact a thoughtful and humane master and an admirable host. Audubon stayed there in 1831 and wrote enthusiastically of Bulow's 'unremitted efforts to make me comfortable, and to promote my researches'. Bulow was even able to keep on good terms with the sullen Seminole Indians, who exchanged fresh venison for whatever they wanted from him. It was agreed throughout north-east Florida that Bulow was a most fortunate young man.

Then, everything went. The Seminole War arrived, and with it, to Bulowville, Major Putnam of St Augustine and a company of militia who called themselves the *Mosquito Roarers*. They had come to protect the plantation from the Seminoles, and Bulow, who felt he had nothing to fear from his venison-suppliers, did not want to be protected and even fired a blank charge from his little cannon at the militia. This would not do, and Major Putnam and his *Mosquito Roarers* seized the place and kept Bulow a prisoner in his own house. (I have taken these facts from *The Valiant Pioneers* by Alice Strickland.) Bulowville was now fortified and was used as a military head-quarters for the whole region. But in the end, the militia, outnumbered by the Seminoles, were ordered to abandon Bulowville, taking all the plantation horses and wagons for their own use and not allowing poor Bulow to remove any of his personal belongings. The Seminoles, howling vengeance on their former friend, came charging in, plundered and burned, and left the plantation the ruin it still is today. And poor John

Joachim Bulow, who had done his best and not wished any real harm to anybody, sailed away from Florida, and shortly afterwards, before he had reached thirty, died in Paris. It is surprising that no American writer, with a taste for savage irony, has given us the Life and Times of John Joachim Bulow. Think what Voltaire or Anatole France could have done with this bitter tale!

Close to the dark ruins of the sugar mill was a hut in which our excellent refreshments were served. As it was very warm in there, many of us took our food and drink outside. There I had some talk with Ken Law, one of the 'cellos, who had been exhibiting, in a room off the foyer of the Auditorium, some charming little pen-and-wash drawings, mostly brought back from the L.S.O.'s tour of the Far East. I had some talk too with a youngish man who was there with the L.S.O. but was actually a freelance, taking the place of one of the members who could not make the trip to Daytona. There were several of these replacements: later I met one extremely intelligent young man—a viola, I think—who was a member of the Philharmonia; and one of the trumpet players, who seemed to vanish when off the platform, was actually Chairman of a rival orchestra. The freelance introduced me to his wife, busy trying to cope with the insistent demands of her small son; and this rather harassed mother, brown and slender, turned out to be on holiday from playing the double-bass with another symphony orchestra—the most unlikely double-bass I ever saw. And earlier I had seen, coming out of the deep shadow of the trees, a magnificent young woman, whose abbreviated costume revealed her as being nearly as dark as a Seminole Indian; and I was surprised, a little later, when this exotic creature spoke to me in the accent of Ealing or Hendon, being yet another orchestra wife.

On the way home, when we had left behind our well-informed but determinedly loquacious guide, who later appeared to be in charge of the whole expedition, I found myself brooding over hospitality and generosity as displayed in Florida and elsewhere in America. (I have visited this country many times.) It is easy to feel overwhelmed by such hospitality and generosity, such immediate kindness to strangers, of a sort rarely experienced by visitors to England—or, for that matter, to most places in Western Europe. (Russia is quite different, and in many respects far more like America.) I don't wish to seem ungrateful—and indeed I have expressed my gratitude over and over again—but as I brooded I seemed to detect a flaw in this gem of hospitality, generosity, kindness to strangers. It tends too often to be ruthless. You are going to be done good to—come hell or high water! This is how we do it here and you're crazy if you don't like it! Come on, man —relax and just have a swell time! *You* are to be entertained, but what all too often won't be entertained is the notion that this may not be your idea of a swell time. So although in one sense you—the visitor who must be kindly treated—are in the centre of the picture, in another sense you yourself, as a person with individual tastes and standards, aren't in the picture at all. So many of the people eager to be hospitable, generous, kind, make no attempt to put themselves in your place, to look at things from your point of view. There is, in short, a want of empathy, a lack of imagination. And I asked myself if it wasn't precisely this underlying weakness, finally allowing ruthlessness to break through, that explains the failure of America in so many parts of the world, where, after what seems like base ingratitude, revolt follows apathy or derision.

2

My old big canvas holdall, which I had taken everywhere because almost anything could be stuffed into it *at the last minute*, had been threatening to lose its handles for some time. That morning, giving my old friend a last sharp tug, I lost handles and holdall for ever. So Jacquetta and I crossed the bridge to the shopping district over the river, to find the luggage store. In charge of it, though her only assistant was a dreamy young girl who appeared to turn round only on the same spot as if she were acting as a lighthouse, was the most energetic and compelling saleswoman I have ever met for some years. Now an American citizen, she had grown up a Pole and had spent some hideous time in a concentration camp. Defying the climate and the local slowed-down style of life, she seemed to be moving and climbing a ladder, taking down bags, offering me bags, opening bags, talking to us and talking on the telephone, all at the same time, in a continuing blur of activity, a montage of high-pressured saleswomanship, never for a second losing her good humour. Finally, inevitably caving in after all that unsuccessful ladder work and shelf-emptying, very dubiously I accepted a case, new to me, that had a canvas side, plaid too, which could be zipped. I didn't believe in it; Jacquetta didn't believe in it; and I doubt if the revolving young-girl-assistant, who never had to assist, believed in it; and we were all wrong, except of course the splendid untiring Polish saleswoman. (And I beg her pardon for having forgotten her name.) Now I know, after Daytona Beach, Martha's Vineyard, Boston, London Airport and Albany and Alveston, that even more can be stuffed into this case than into my canvas holdall—and at the last minute too.

Our friend Mary McLemore and her English professor at Stetson University had persuaded me to give a talk there early this evening. So the McLemores drove me to De Land, about twenty-five miles away, where Stetson, not a bad-looking institution, is to be found. The lecture room was crowded; the audience was attentive and warmly appreciative; the talk was a great success—much discussed afterwards, I was told—and the column in next day's local paper was boldly headed: *Priestley Wit Shines In Speech*. Only one person —at least to my certain knowledge—disliked it, and that was Witty Shining Priestley himself. Not that I was humbugging them. What I said I believed; I told them nothing I wasn't prepared to act upon myself; there was no lying, no hypocrisy, no nonsense meant to tickle and please; but I didn't satisfy myself, feeling empty within, performing rather than releasing urgent talk. I was not unlike the L.S.O. with Mozart, playing him but not from the inside, where so much could be illuminated.

Moreover, I was back in time only for the second part of Ashkenazy's recital—alas, missing his two Beethoven sonatas, the *Moonlight* and the A Major Op. 101, which I thought he might have left until after the intermission. What I had instead were the Chopin *Barcarolle* and Schumann's *Carnaval*. Both were beautifully played, but I don't happen to be particularly fond of the Chopin and *Carnaval* irritated me. Apparently I have now seen too many years to find any fascination in *Carnaval*, which makes me feel I am at a fancy-dress ball and staying too long. There was a time, before two wars, when I loved its elaborate fantastication, just as I loved the poetry of Swinburne and much else that I no longer need; but now I would prefer to escape from *Carnaval*, even with an Ashkenazy playing it. And I would have felt sad about this evening's recital if I hadn't known that I would soon be hearing Ashkenazy playing with the orchestra.

3

The day of the Seventh Orchestral Concert seemed to me unusually hot. I crawled down to the beach in the morning but then retreated before its huge glare. However, just raised above it was a wooden house with a small white balcony and white steps outside and its walls a fading and peeling emerald green. It was probably little more than twenty years old, but between two new and fancy motels it looked like a survivor, plain and sensible, from antiquity. Moreover, its mottled and dimming emerald walls were tempting. So, sweating and watery-eyed, I made a quick pencil sketch of it, together with a few colour notes, and then in the afternoon, refusing to go out again, I did a paint of sorts, mostly from memory, of this house and part of the surrounding scene. It wasn't good. I have just looked at it again, trying to decide which sketches were worth framing, and it still isn't good—in fact, quite bad.

However, it swallowed an hour or two of the long hot day, all the longer and hotter because I was eagerly looking forward to the·night's concert: Berlioz's *Corsaire* Overture; Rachmaninoff's Second Concerto, with Ashkenazy the soloist; Schumann's Fourth Symphony, the D Minor; and Strauss's *Till Eulenspiegel*; a fine fat programme, under Kertesz, who had just returned from conducting in Chicago. But in trying to give the evening a good start, we gave it through no fault of our own a bad one. We had carefully booked a table, at a restaurant fairly near the Auditorium, for 7.15, which left us ample time to enjoy whatever food and wine we could order there. We arrived there at 7.15 on the dot, only to find that no table had been kept for us, the place being quite crowded. The proprietress, who is supposed to offer her patrons a warm personal welcome, kept us standing there for several minutes, then muttered something about too many

[80

people having come along, after which she scuttled off in the direction of the kitchen. If she had told us over the phone she couldn't guarantee to keep a table for us, we could have gone earlier and claimed one. But she had accepted the reservation without making any real attempt to honour it. Later, exchanging notes on local customs, we found it to be common form here to accept reservations, whether for meals or hair-dos, without bothering to keep them. And now, with time running out, we had to find another restaurant, which we did, and it was almost full and almost impenetrable in its semi-darkness. Rather foolishly, perhaps, we ordered 'hot sea-food platters', and after a wait of twenty minutes or so, with time now galloping away, they came and were indeed quite good, but with everything so barbarously piled up on the large platters that we felt we had just ten minutes to eat our way through Battersea Fun Fair.

Hot, anxious, with half our shares of lobster already threatening the next twelve hours, we hurried to the Auditorium and sank into our seats, our tempers not improved by the fact that the large audience, nearly a full house, was as usual taking its time to settle down. I took it out on the Auditorium. 'It's not badly proportioned,' I muttered to Jacquetta, 'and it's reasonably cool and comfortable, but even so, for my money, it's still a seaside pavilion. So what in the hell is the L.S.O. doing here?' Whatever it might be doing, the orchestra would have to do it without its concert master, John Georgiadis (we learnt later he had collected a virus and some temporary deafness from the swimming pool), and his deputy, Hans Geiger, one of the few older men among the strings, took the leader's bow. Probably glad to be out of Chicago, Kertesz came on, chubby and cheerful, and then we were off, hurrying and scurrying this time with Berlioz.

Apart from its calm-sea *Adagio* section, *Le Corsaire*, which I had heard Beecham play more than once, must be one of the most hurrying-scurrying overtures ever written. And Berlioz

81]

in his corsairing mood was just a slice of red meat to these boys, from the first running-up-and-down-stairs of the strings and woodwind to the final blaze of brass. I never heard it played better, not even under Beecham, though he used to add a touch of his own, out of his almost insolent showmanship, by moving away at once, after the last great chord from the trombones, as if about to take a stroll.

Jumping from the first to the final item on the programme, I will now add that I doubt if I have ever heard a better performance of Strauss's *Till Eulenspiegel*, very much a showpiece for a virtuoso orchestra. It is a work I have listened to over and over again, both in live performances and recordings. Grumpy as I might have been feeling, it seemed to me that even the Vienna Philharmonic under Von Karajan offered nothing more enchanting than the L.S.O.'s opening impression of these 'merry pranks', with Barry Tuckwell's horn theme at once meltingly gay and yet melancholy and Roger Lord and the rest of the woodwind perky and mischievous and still beautiful. Though this performance followed (as we shall see) a sharp disappointment, I was commanded by sheer confident virtuosity to revel in it—and revel I did.

The disappointment was not the Rachmaninoff concerto, though this had its faults. Kertesz is an excellent musician but in one respect he is inferior as yet to several of our older English conductors: he is not a tactful and accommodating conductor for a soloist. Unless I was badly placed for recognizing a satisfactory balance between soloists and the orchestra—and perhaps I might have been better able to judge it up in the balcony—I couldn't help feeling more than once that he came down too heavily with his men, making his soloists fight their accompaniments. This seemed to me noticeable in the big cossacks-come-riding passage towards the end of the first movement of the Rachmaninoff. (Incidentally, I wished Ashkenazy had been playing No. 3 or even the much undervalued No. 4.) In such fortissimo passages, Ashkenazy

[82

has a trick of rocking on his stool and appearing to snatch at the great loud chords. This led to much argument, some of it in print but mostly in talk, about his sheer physical ability to crash out this big stuff against a heavy orchestral accompaniment. Had he the necessary strength and weight? Should he be told to avoid these big, severely-taxing concertos? My own conclusion was that Ashkenazy's lack of height and bulk was deceptive, that he is in fact quite strongly built, and that the idea that he needed more muscle for Rachmaninoff's cossacks came from the L.S.O.'s over-enthusiastic support and from his own rocking-and-apparently-snatching mannerism, which he would now be wise to discard. The slow movement, which to my mind offers us a more essential and precious distillation of Rachmaninoff 1900–1901 than the other two movements, was of course exquisitely played.

No, the great disappointment so far as I was concerned was the Schumann Fourth Symphony, the D Minor. It was all the more bitter because from the time I had first looked through the Festival programme, I had been waiting impatiently for the performance of this symphony. I don't know if I am revealing now my own ignorance or a fairly recent change of fashion, but it is a fact that before the Second War I had never once heard this work, not even in a recording. The first live performance was under Von Karajan, who may have played a few tricks with the orchestration but did at the end lift the audience out of their seats, cheering. After that I listened often to the two recordings I possess, for this symphony had for a time a curious fascination for me, quite different from the moderate enjoyment I found in Schumann's other three symphonies. And this was not because it was highly original, ahead of its time, movement flowing into movement without a break, themes magically changing and yet remaining themselves in essence. After all, I am much closer to literature and psychology than I am to musicology. (But even so, I have ears to hear with and, given a little time, can recognise what is happening to a

83]

theme.) In this symphony, it seems to me, Schumann is belatedly expressing and then crying farewell to the whole German Romantic movement, to the darkly enchanted forests, the dream castles, the iron knights, the innocent tender maidens, the magic potions and witches and sorcerers, the fairy-tale towns, and far away in the sky the faint gleams and lilac shadows of illusory Arabian palaces. (Purple passage, eh? Yeah—and so what? This is the old German Romantic movement.) And there is something else—or so it has always seemed to me—and that is a menacing hint, perhaps rather more than a hint, of that madness which is soon to take hold of Schumann and destroy him. Consider, for example, that wonderful mysterious introduction to the final movement, and then its false endings, its terrible blares of brass, sending the strings hurrying from *presto* to *prestissimo*, hell-for-leather somewhere—anywhere.

So now my favourite orchestra was to play this *Symphonische Phantasie*—Schumann's original name for it, afterwards dropped. Just as I had been looking forward to the dinner in the French restaurant and then couldn't even sit down in the place, so too all my eager expectancy with the Schumann ended in dismay. I have already suggested that some works—the Mozart symphonies, for example—were played but not really interpreted, not illuminated from the inside. But I felt that the Schumann was not even played, not even decently lit up from the outside. Those bewitching triplets for solo violin, in the middle section of the *Romanza*, could hardly be heard at all; they were drowned like so many unwanted kittens; and this also meant that Schumann's brilliant modification of their theme, in the trio of the Scherzo, might pass unnoticed. And the finale, which could have been written to be performed after more than a century by the L.S.O., sounded half-hearted, curiously botched and smudged. Nor can it be said that the players, after their 'shrimp boils' and fun on the beach, were tired or bored, because as soon as the Schumann was shovelled

[84

away they took us at once, with their Strauss, into an Ali Baba cave of jewels. Perhaps I ought to have had it out with them, demanding to know why they ruined my Schumann for me, but I never did. I am—and I don't care how much evidence there is to contradict me—a sensitive delicate-minded man.

4

All that afternoon before the Eighth Orchestral Concert, we had a thunderstorm that just went on and on and on, never attempting anything spectacular but never leaving us until early evening—a determined bore of a thunderstorm. And it produced in me a leaden feeling, a boiled-milk flavour, I hadn't known for a long time. I was alone in a house that wasn't my own house, where I can always find something I want to do. I couldn't go out because of the storm. I couldn't work, I couldn't play. I had books still unread but there was something in the atmosphere that made continous reading very difficult—indeed, impossible. So for once—and this is so unusual that it really was remarkable—I was fathoms deep in boredom. As we used to say in the West Riding, I was 'fast with myself'. Even the devil, generally so hard at work with idle hands, ignored me. In the unreal thunderstorm light, I wandered from room to room like a ghost that no longer frightened anybody, a bore of a bored ghost. I kept going out into the wet garden to see if the evening paper had arrived. This was delivered to us, some time between 4.30 and 6.30, by a boy on a bicycle who didn't stop but flung the folded paper, held by a rubber band, somewhere in our direction, so that it might land in the garden, on the steps going down from the front door, or even in the garage below. This local evening paper always had some Festival news or criticism on its front page, but even so I wasn't usually eager to pounce upon it; yet now, so deeply sunk was I in boredom that I must have gone out looking for it—in bedroom slippers too—at least a dozen times. For once I was tasting life, as if it were a gigantic saltless four-minute-boiled egg, after the melancholy fashion of so many of our fellow mortals.

But who cares what I was feeling on Friday, 28th July,

1967? I do. And you should do, if you have read so far in this book, which is clearly intended for a fairly large middle section of people between the musical experts of various sorts and all those who simply don't want to listen to classical music. The critics—and I am not blaming them—attend concerts in a kind of vacuum, where there is no weather, there are no moods, no shoe pinches them and indigestion is unknown: here they are and here is the music, and that is all. And the people at the other extreme remain in their outer darkness with *Musak* and its faint lakes and cascades of golden syrup. You and I, my friends, eager to listen to music but aware of ourselves and the world around us, are the people represented here. Certainly this is all about *me*, but then this is my chronicle and on this level of thought and feeling couldn't be anybody else's. (But a lot of people, both out there and back here, have said 'Are you writing a *novel* about it then?') Let me put it like this. I took the trouble, risking considerable expense, to remain a month in Daytona Beach, which would never be my first choice for a summer holiday, to be close to a particularly fine orchestra when it was far away from home and coming up with concert after concert, *not* taking place in a vacuum; and before we have done we shall take a long serious look together at the L.S.O.—and indeed at the whole immensely difficult task of maintaining a symphony orchestra at a high standard. (See the last chapter—but, please, not yet.) I may possibly enjoy writing about myself, but what I am really after here—with, at last, an okay word—is the *ambience*. And now, having conjured what might have been a preface into the middle of this book, I can go to the concert. But not, remember, a concert given in some spacemen's testing chamber, clean out of our atmosphere, but in a place all too human and on the evening of this particular day.

It was Goldberg's turn to conduct. He is a master violinist, a charming man, and good, no doubt, with a chamber ensemble, but neither inspired nor inspiring, I would say, as a conductor of a symphony orchestra. There was no big flashy stuff, ninety-men-in-a-frenzy, on his programme. We never came nearer to it than Hindemith's *Concert Music for Brass and Strings*, composed in 1930 and commissioned by the Boston Symphony to celebrate—if that term can be used for Hindemith—its fiftieth anniversary. Perhaps I ought to have a special feeling for Hindemith as he was born not long after I was; but somehow I can never pump it up. I have listened to him with some enjoyment—as I did on this occasion, when the L.S.O. strings and brass were very fine—but he tends to make me feel he is standing me a drink, probably a gigantic stein of *Löwenbrau*, rather than offering me a memorable experience. I never want to spend any time alone with his music.

I have spent plenty of time alone with Haydn and Schubert, whose respective Symphonies No. 88 in G and No. 3 in D formed part of this programme. The Haydn was conscientiously performed but didn't convince me that the L.S.O. might now be *with* the Eighteenth Century. Schubert's jolly little symphony was written when he was eighteen, together with much else. Not that I am one of those who think of Schubert himself as a jolly little chap. Little he was—under five-foot-two—and he could be jolly enough with his friends, though so shy elsewhere he would enter a room almost sideways; but he was no 'chap' but one of the most gifted human beings who ever existed, all 'a wonder and a wild desire'. To read his story while remembering his music is to feel a weight on the heart. We don't deserve such beings. It is they who must come to us from other and better planets.

Another of these visitants we earthborn creatures tried to hammer into the ground was of course Mozart, whose Horn Concerto No. 2 Goldberg gave us with Barry Tuckwell as the soloist. I already knew, from the recording, that while Tuckwell plays the whole thing superbly well, his own peculiarly personal tone, further removed from us and more mysterious than other horns, is best heard in the opening *Allegro maestoso*

[88

movement; and now I will venture something that I can only hope will not annoy a splendid musician who is also a pleasant companion. Tuckwell has been playing in symphony orchestras, five altogether, since he was fifteen, and by now, when he is already a widely-acclaimed soloist, he may well be tired of taking his seat with the other three horns and waiting so often for some magical little passage he can make his own. He cannot be blamed if by this time he wants to leave behind that crowd of ninety-odd and move off to be his own master. Yet it seems to me—and I can't drag anybody else into this— that the horn is such an instrument that, no matter what virtuosity is brought to it in concertos and chamber music—and Tuckwell's cannot be doubted or faulted—its true magic, its voice calling from lost woods and happier days, is best heard and remembered when it comes to us from the orchestra. Tuckwell plainly seen is a magnificent instrumentalist; but it is when he is hardly visible up there, one voice among so many, that he is the master of enchantment.

5

This Saturday morning saw us setting out on an expedition
that had been planned some days ahead. It was not simple
tourism; music came into it. We were on our way to visit all
that was left of the Solano orange grove, once the property of
the composer, my distinguished fellow-Bradfordian, Frederick
Delius. Our guide was Ronald Moore, the clarinet player and
one of the L.S.O. directors, who had been up there before and
had been exchanging letters (she had no telephone) with Mrs
McFarland, an elderly widow, now the present owner of the
property. And of course Moore knew how to find the place; I
suspect that without him we might be still looking for it. So
off we went, due north, with the Ronald Moores and their
family in the first car, Roger Lord (principal oboe), his wife
Madeleine and son Jeremy, travelling behind with us. After an
hour or so of smooth motoring, we turned off and bounced our
way, through denser and denser vegetation, along a very
narrow and deeply-rutted dirt road. We might have been ex-
ploring the upper reaches of the Orinoco. However, Mrs
McFarland's house, in a clearing near the river, was quite
comfortable; she was glad to see us; and fine preparations for
lunch, with local shrimps the centrepiece, went forward, with
the help of Elizabeth Moore and Madeleine Lord. I wanted to
do a paint, on or near the river, so Mrs McFarland, wiry,
energetic and delightful, led the way for Jacquetta and me,
carrying a hoe through the undergrowth because of rattle-
snakes. Delius's own original shack was no longer here, having
been taken down and rebuilt, by an enthusiastic Mrs Richmond,
at the university in Jacksonville, which now runs an annual
Delius Festival every February. (No steaming July-August
festival, please note, for Jacksonville!) But here, an expanse of
polished pewter in the noon sunlight, was the St John's

[90

River, three-and-a-half miles wide. This was the river Delius had stared at for months and had finally set its life to music.

The nearest jetty was almost falling to pieces, so much rotten wood, but it was possible to go out along it, for some coloured men and boys were fishing at the covered end of it. Along went the intrepid Mrs McFarland and the equally intrepid Jacquetta; but they were sure-footed lightweights and I wasn't—moreover, I was carrying all my painting gear and in the heat and glitter I felt anything but sure-footed—so halfway along I stopped and then retreated, settling down at the land end of it to try a sketch. It was hellishly hot; the biters set about me; and there was too much Spanish Moss, which I find almost impossible to paint. However, I daubed away—a few rotten planks of the jetty in the bottom foreground, a tree trunk or two on the left, some curtaining of Spanish Moss above, and in the middle and to the right the empty river. When I was called to lunch I looked with disgust at what I had done, and Jacquetta didn't care for it, but since then, well away from its place of origin, it has somehow pulled itself together; and when I showed it not long ago to Joan Chissell, who had also been up there, she gave a little cry of instant recognition, remembering at once the very place where I had been sitting.

One of the rewards of this hobby—we can ignore creative art here—is that when you try to draw or paint a landscape you enter into a kind of symbiotic relationship with it. You may be busy with your brushes and much too hot and pestered and bitten by insects, as I was, but part of your mind is soon invaded by thoughts and feelings arising out of the essential character of the scene. With its dense jungle undergrowth, its live oaks and pines and cypresses (with hardly an orange tree to be found now) hidden by the sinister curtains and festoons of grey-beard-and-giant-spider-webbing of Spanish Moss, and its vast, silent and empty river, the whole scene had an air of huge melancholy decay, suggesting not the gay young Fred Delius who had gone there in 1884 but the austere, blind and paralysed recluse of Grez-sur-Loing. As if, you might say, the region had kept pace with him, deepening into sombre decay as he had done.

We are apt to assume that every place is livelier and more bustling than it used to be. This is not true of the region here, this former plantation country on the west bank of the St John's River. Willing to try almost anything to escape from Bradford and the family wool business, Delius took over this Solano orange grove, together with another young rebel Bradfordian, Charles Douglas. (This may seem an odd enterprise, but there was in fact a little boom in Florida orange-growing in the 1880s.) Douglas soon fled, and there is no doubt that Delius did spend a month or two alone, brooding over the river, going out night-fishing with the coloured men, giving an ear to their singing and strumming. And out of these memories of tunes and rhythms and odd harmonies unknown in Bradford then, there came much of his earliest music; and indeed it could be argued that at least a suggestion of melancholy-exotic-Florida-brooding remained in his music to the end. But he did not in fact spend as much time alone at Solano as, long afterwards, he declared he did. Those jetties, now falling to pieces, were in constant use during the 1880s, when there were many plantations along that mud-flatted bank and everybody went to and from Jacksonville by water, with the St John's River like another Mississippi. One plantation neighbour, Mrs Bell, was musical and a friend of Grieg (Delius met him a little later, in Leipzig), and she and Delius were much in each other's company, and after he had left Florida they corresponded for many years. He discovered a professional musician in Jacksonville—Ward, a young organist from Brooklyn, visiting Florida for his health—and he spent more and more time in Jacksonville and less and less at Solano, eventually leaving it entirely to go to Danvill, Virginia. There he became 'Professor Delius, teacher of music'

[92

and worked hard, with thoughts of Leipzig in mind. Altogether Delius was in Florida less than a year, returning only for one brief visit afterwards, and now his orange grove has vanished. But the river still flows through the dusk in his music.

When I was painting or mooching around after lunch or huddling down in the car on the way back, I kept thinking about Delius, who walked along Manningham Lane, Bradford, over thirty years before I did. A puzzling figure; though, as Cardus rightly tells us, a more original and stronger composer than he is generally supposed to be. (And Eric Fenby's admirable accounts of Delius at work, dictating a score out of his blindness, don't suggest a dilettante—anything but.) It is hard to bring into the focus of one life, one personality, the familiar—perhaps over-familiar—image of the stricken recluse of Grez-sur-Loing, austere, disdainful, almost the aristocrat, and the good-looking and high-spirited young man from Bradford (accent an' all) who hunted alligators here, went floating down to Jacksonville, and afterwards roistered in Leipzig. Much has been written about his 'Englishness', but surely he is not English as Elgar so essentially is. Elgar was hardly ever out of the sight and smell of Worcestershire, whereas Delius spent almost the whole of his adult life outside England. True, he was born and he grew up in the West Riding, but if his music ever suggests its stone walls, sleety moors and tall chimneys, it has never done so when I have been listening. No doubt he is hauntingly *nostalgic*. (I take this to be the most overworked term of our recent time; thus, a novel of mine, *Lost Empires*, about life in the music halls, had *nostalgic* pasted on to it, simply because I set its action back in 1913–14, when there seems to me not a glimmer of true nostalgia in any page of it.) Certainly, again and again, Delius makes us share his nostalgia. But nostalgia—for where—for what? And before we reply, we must remember he sounded this deeply personal note long before paralysis and blindness struck him. He might be said to have been nostalgic before he had had anything to be nostalgic about. Again, we have read a lot about his love of Nature, his closeness to her, which he is always trying to express. But is he? Other composers, I feel, have brought me much closer to the natural scene than Delius has ever done. Even in one of his more robust works, *Brigg Fair*, we never attend a fair but seem to be drawn into aching memories of some vanished long-lost fair, rising at the end to cries that have more anguish than joy in them. I cannot find in his work, original and quite powerful within its narrow limits, any simple extraverted lover of Nature. His nostalgia is for something somewhere that never was—not in the West Riding, Norway, Florida, Germany, France, not here at all. And just as so many artists, moving towards an early death, have worked prodigiously in feverish haste, as if their unconscious knew they had so little time, so possibly Delius in every creative mood felt a faint foreshadowing of those years of paralysis and blindness that were waiting for him. And if not that, then there is a master key to him still missing.

These thoughts, such as they are, belong to here and now in this expression of them, but they are more or less the same that nagged at me before and after thanking Mrs McFarland —perhaps my favourite Floridan—and then leaving her alone in her remote house, with the Spanish Moss creeping towards it. Back we bounced—and why not some alliteration here?— along the rutted road, through what would pass as an unexplored jungle on the widest cinema screen. The usual thunderstorm claimed the last of the afternoon; we reached the main road with lightning and fierce drumming rods of rain; we splashed through what seemed to be a series of new lakes on our way to Daytona and the evening's concert. And it might well have offered us a little Delius, but of course it didn't.

6

Rather an odd programme had been arranged for this Ninth Orchestral Concert, probably on something-for-everybody lines. The first half was to be all Beethoven—the *Egmont* overture and then the Violin Concerto; the second half all Tschaikowsky—his Sixth Symphony, our old friend the *Pathetic*. And it had a new conductor, Jascha Horenstein, whom I had already seen around, and indeed we had exchanged some scraps of talk. His name and excellent reputation I had known for many years, of course, but oddly enough I had never attended any concert of his, nor seen him perform before. He is not tall but he has a large head and a long and rather melancholy face, out of which comes—or so it seemed to me, though he may have other tones—a gentle melancholy voice. And on this brief acquaintance he suggested a minor Chekhov character, perhaps a doctor arriving in the second act. However, this was not his platform personality. There he has an odd style of conducting, raising and lowering his arms straight up and down, looking from behind like a man doing exercises; but he knows his scores and his business, obviously concentrates on the broad development of the work on hand, and, unlike the younger conductors, avoids turning to this section and that fussing away with entrance cues and signals. But then of course he is an old hand and has been taking charge of big orchestras since 1923. Some of the players here, who enjoyed him, told me that when he is displeased by the sound he is hearing he immediately covers his nose with his left hand, which in effect is crying 'You stink!'

There was nothing wrong with the *Egmont* overture except that as soon as it began it suffered some competition from a deaf old couple in the front row, who shouted at each other as if they were in their own back room. Nobody quietened them, but perhaps they noticed the faces of the nearest violinists, for after a minute or two they stopped shouting. So this interruption, the only one I remember in the Auditorium, didn't last long, but it left us giggling a little inside, unsettled, not quite ready to admire in all earnestness the combined solemn heroics of Goethe and Ludwig van Beethoven.

Goldberg played the Violin Concerto, and of course played it supremely well. It came out small and pure, all the smaller and purer because he went back to Joachim's original cadenza in place of the familiar one by Kreisler. Goldberg and Horenstein first played this Beethoven together, with the Warsaw Philharmonic, some time between thirty-five and forty years ago, and since then had shared many concerts; so Horenstein, knowing his man, handled the orchestra very skilfully; but, for all that, there were a few moments when it was hard to avoid the impression that a small and very good boy had allowed himself to be enticed into a game being played by big rough boys. That this is the pre-eminently noble and beautiful work we are always told it is, the most spiritual of all violin concertos, I have no doubt—and all of this was revealed again—but, even so, I for one am not sorry that other composers have gone to work for this instrument on a lower level, where fiddlers have wine and women in mind and don't refuse a small helping of *schmalz* and close their eyes and sway and show off. I am not against a faint suggestion of charlatanry in the violin as a solo instrument, a Paganini touch.

After wading through the river of Coca-cola, to sniff the night air, we returned to the second part of the concert and Tschaikowsky's *Pathetic* symphony. I had not heard a live performance of this work for some time, but my acquaintance with it goes back to my early youth, when, after hearing several performances of it, I used to borrow a piano arrangement from the Free Library and struggle and thump away. (Even if I had been able to play it, any piano arrangement would have still been a nonsense.) Horenstein and the L.S.O.,

[96

Jascha Horenstein rehearsing Beethoven's Ninth Symphony.

Ashkenazy taking a class of students.

Geoffrey Gilbert with some of his woodwind students.

Barry Tuckwell with some of his group.

The tall blonde is leader of the Students' Orchestra.

A very attractive
student of the 'cello.

Sir Arthur Bliss is lending a hand at the pool.

John Pigneguy (horn) and Chris Green ('cello) gazing at a heap of fried chicken at the Wild West rodeo.

The Ashkenazy family after a bathe.

Jacquetta is carrying J.B.P.'s painting portfolio.

Sam Artis (violin) and Alex Lindsay (leader of the second violins) have caught some big fish.

A break during morning rehearsal.

The last surviving orange tree from Delius's Solano Grove.

The Michael Winfield (oboe) family in their apartment.

Mrs Roger Lord and the Ronald Moore (clarinet) family at Solano Grove.

Jascha Horenstein with his old friend Szymon Goldberg.

while giving full value to the music, to the symphony, made me feel that they had made up their minds not to overdo the thing, not to offer us a psychedelic Saturday night, not to tempt us to rush out and commit suicide, so that I have heard strings, not so formidable as those of the L.S.O., cut deeper into the marzipan melancholy of the last movement. And for my part, I was all in favour of this comparatively cool treatment. This is a piece of music—and in its way a very considerable piece of music—and not the script for a tearful orgy.

The truth is, Tschaikowsky's brother, Modeste, did him more harm than good when he called this Sixth Symphony the *Pathetic*, turning it into a kind of suicides' musical textbook. Not that Tschaikowsky's own life was entirely free from morbid and hysterical passages; perhaps at no time did he successfully avoid them. After all, he seriously threatened to commit suicide himself more than once, and married a young woman, when he didn't really want a woman at all, because *she* announced she was ready to kill herself if he scorned her. He lived, we may well say, in a *Pathetic Symphony* atmosphere. But for many of us, the label defeats the music—at least that of the first and fourth movements. *Oh—you're going to be pathetic, are you?* we mutter. *Well, we'll see about that.* And so we stiffen ourselves against it, harden our hearts, and jeer when we ought to be weeping. And it is not, as some people think, because we are afraid of pathos, of losing our hold on our emotions. I have seen too many clever people's eyes filled with tears, in the theatre or the cinema, to believe that.

We are softer not harder than the Victorians. They were so tough, in a tough world, that they wanted, they needed, a good cry, the men even more than the women, to wash them out of their toughness. Jeffrey, for example, who could hardly think of Dickens's Little Nell without bursting into tears, must have passed sentences in his courts that would now make our hair stand on end. So we guard ourselves against determined assaults on our emotions. We don't ban pathos but insist on

97]

its being rather dry, brief, terse, a by-product, not in the main line of production. As Chesterton pointed out, we dislike Dickens's pathos because he tried to make it as expansive as humour. We object to the death of Paul Dombey, not because we are so callous about children, but, on the contrary, because we don't like to see Dickens enjoying himself, putting one through a slow-motion wringing machine. And so far as it is labelled *Pathetic* and is apparently about to ask us to contemplate suicide, we are on our guard, ready with a quip, a sneer, against Tschaikowsky's Sixth Symphony, which may be inferior to his Fifth or his Fourth (my own preference) or possibly *Manfred* too, but remains a rich and pleasing composition—that is, if you take it fairly coolly and freshly, as Horenstein and the L.S.O. and I for one did, that Saturday night.

I seem to remember our going to one of the better parties afterwards, and, unless I have my nights confused, having some talk among others with Alan Jenkins, alert and beaming after coping with his tuba. I said I had something of a passion for this grave and noble instrument, and then he told me that last year a young girl here really had been gripped by this passion I was pretending to have, for she had begged him to explain everything about the tuba and then had sat close to him at rehearsals, listening to and watching closely every sound and every move he made. Perhaps by this time she is actually playing a tuba somewhere. For myself, if I were not too old and fat and idle, I should like to learn enough of the tuba so that if I could find one of these new *Minus One* records meant for it—for these records give you all the parts except the one you want to play yourself—I could enjoy many a happy afternoon with the record-player full on and its sound deeply and nobly completed by my tuba. And this was the last fancy of the day, a long day, beginning with the expedition to Solano, but a good one.

[98

7

Some Sundays are more Sundayish than others, and this was one of them. The morning—my morning, certainly—was frittered away. We had invited the Goldbergs to lunch and had decided they should have a typical English Sunday lunch —roast beef and two vegetables and apple tart—and only reflected when it was too late that this was what hotels and restaurants here were putting on the table every day. But the Goldbergs, though delightful people, are not food-and-drink types. Szymon Goldberg is intensely dedicated to his music: a deeply serious character with high ideals, which he is not afraid of mentioning as most of us English are. He does not understand us. (Or he didn't then. Now he may if he really has settled in London.) He finds us puzzling and teasing. This came out when he was talking about the L.S.O. He said he greatly admired the orchestra and loved to listen to it, but found himself at odds with it during rehearsals. The younger violinists and 'cellists insisted upon making silly little jokes and giggling among themselves. With his intense devotion and high ideals, to him even a first rehearsal was a solemn occasion, to be elevated well above any sort of nonsense and horseplay; and though he knew that these same young men would give a splendid performance, it disturbed him, almost pained him, that they should behave so childishly during rehearsal. It was not how music should be made. I told him that there was in the English character a certain superficial flippancy and irresponsibility. We can be serious, I continued, but unlike so many Central Europeans we don't *enjoy* being serious. I might have added that we live in fear of being bored and being boring, in dread of somehow being press-ganged into a conference of European intellectuals or American social scientists. And I must add here that if I have suggested that

Goldberg is a humourless prig, then I have gone entirely wrong, for in company he is a twinkling, quietly humorous man who can offer or take a joke—unless, of course, the company has been assembled for the almost sacerdotal ceremony of making music.

This was the afternoon of the *Hungarian Banquet Honoring Istvan Kertesz*, for which we had taken tickets for the whole household. The other three having gone ahead, Jacquetta and I arrived late, full of lunch and not prepared to take a banquet seriously. I had imagined us sitting at small tables, all round an open space, and enjoying a glass or two of wine while Hungarian dancers, gipsy fiddlers, and the rest, turned that open space into some sort of Magyar camp. And what we found came no closer to that vision than a Trades Union Congress could do. Into a huge dining room at the Voyager Beach Motel, itself a gigantic establishment, several hundred warm people had been packed, all sitting at long tables. On each side of Kertesz, at the top table, was a menacing line of speakers, reciters, singers, ready to stay there for hours and hours. A spicy Hungarian first course was being served, all right for a banquet and dead wrong for anybody who had already lunched. It had been announced beforehand that many 'colorful Magyar folk costumes' would be worn, and I did see a few of them, all containing solid matrons who somehow looked very American, Moms in the wrong clothes. The crowded dining room was now warmer—and spicier. The programme, beginning with an *Invocation*, a *Proclamation*, then *Introductions*, looked as if it might bore its way clean through into the evening. And delighted though we were that the excellent smiling Kertesz should receive so many tributes from his fellow Hungarians, we crept away. Later we were told that we had been among those given a public welcome by one of the speakers, but this didn't make me feel ashamed. I don't care about public welcomes but always respond amiably to private welcomes, and these we had not had. And anyhow,

[100

we couldn't see ourselves sitting there throughout the afternoon, refusing course after course but being baked in a slow oven ourselves, unable to move, playing rabbit to the stoat of that ruthless programme.

Back in the house I remained in a kind of Sabbath stupor, among a litter of Sunday papers, while Jacquetta went across to the river to photograph the sailing races between townsfolk and the L.S.O. men. (Last year we won the cup; this year they did. Decadence again?) But some time between tea and supper, steeling and burnishing the will, I crawled up to my typewriter, and spent an hour at it doing what would have been about five minutes' work at home. After supper, finally abandoning the litter of papers, we tried to get some news on television. But the set, probably resenting our neglect of it, gave us nothing but glimpses of baseball, patent medicine ads, and a selection of jiggling abstract patterns. If there was a party that night, we didn't go to it; we went to bed. And with no music lingering in our ears.

Fourth Movement

poco a poco bizzaramente

THE last week—and Jacquetta went off early to catch a plane to Miami, on her way to the Everglades. She had been exchanging letters and telephone messages with the National Park people down there, for the past ten days or so. Though the name *Everglades* has long had a certain fascination for me, I decided against going; we both felt that the least I could do was to remain in Daytona Beach. This being the last week, things would now begin to move one way or another. Either they would tighten up, preparing for the climax, or they would loosen and shred out, like a fabric not closely woven. No doubt they were tightening up for the orchestra, now rehearsing several large works for the latter part of the week, among them Beethoven's Ninth; and for all their astounding energy many of the players, having had too much music, too much sun-and-games, too much late-night hospitality, must have been wilting a little, even though nobody complained when I talked to them during the morning's coffee-break. For me, on the other hand, things were loosening and shredding out; I didn't feel as closely *with it* as I had done earlier; I wasn't quite entirely there; my mind began to wander away from Daytona Beach, the Festival, Florida.

I would leave the Auditorium, after the break in the rehearsal, and stroll—and I am not by nature or habit a stroller but these hot mornings had taught me to slow myself down—towards my favourite cross-street, Seabreeze. There I could replenish my stock of the only cigars in the town that were worth smoking. I never knew their name but they were

[102

supposed to be hand-made and they had little curly tails, and they were to be bought on Seabreeze. At the same time I would buy a few more small packets of tobacco. I had some good tobacco but in order to make it last I would buy this other stuff. The packets themselves were wonderfully and most temptingly various on their outsides. They would be Old English or Ould Irish, tremendously outdoors or most snugly indoors, illustrated by attractive little pictures; but all this variety vanished as soon as each packet was opened. It always seemed to me exactly the same tobacco—always *mild and aromatic* when I prefer my tobacco not to be either mild or aromatic—and obviously almost all the originality and creative energy of the manufacturers had not gone into the blending of the tobacco but into the labelling and packaging, the cunning names, the attractive little pictures. It was the ad-men and salesmen, not the tobacco blenders, who were directing the enterprise. And I mention this because it is a good example of what has gone wrong—and is going wronger —in American life, and of what is now being widely imitated in Britain and most of Western Europe. It is a bad trend enthusiastically adopted by the 'trendy'. We are increasingly bamboozled by the outside of the package.

The only music I heard was provided by Roger Lord, principal oboe of the L.S.O. for some years, who was per-forming with the Iowa String Quartet and gave us the Mozart Oboe Quartet, K.370, and Britten's *Fantasy for Oboe and Strings*, a very early work—Opus 2, no more—that begins and ends splendidly but seems to get lost in the middle. Lord's playing of both works was very fine indeed, and I was delighted to be able to tell him so, over a drink or two in that dim bar of his hotel, the Daytona Plaza, where we had some general talk too, all the more valuable because Lord is an exceptionally intelligent and sensitive type of orchestral player, who avoids and deplores what we might call 'symphonic politics'. But the notice of the concert, in the evening paper

103]

next day, returned me to the talk I had had with Steinberg about English woodwind playing: 'Lord is a disciple of the English school of oboe playing,' this local critic wrote, 'that insists on a thin parlous tone and a wide uncontrolled vibrato. I confess I don't really enjoy his performances, but acknowledge that his impeccable taste and musicianship help a lot.' But does such a notice help a lot? And how can an unpleasing tone be reconciled with impeccable taste and musicianship? Clearly, they don't like our woodwind playing over there, and while I don't denounce their accepted style, which of course is European in origin and belongs to the total-mellow-sound tradition, I think their attitude of mind is intolerant and wrong. There is room for more than one style of woodwind playing, just as there is room for more than one style of orchestral playing in general. There are several great European and American orchestras that can produce a total tone, at once massive, rich, smooth, almost like a gigantic slab of milk chocolate, that the L.S.O. cannot achieve, and indeed doesn't want to achieve, if only because it is after something else. But once the L.S.O. has really identified itself with a piece of music—and is not, as I have suggested here, merely playing it—then, risking any danger of appearing to show off, to be a bit brash, to seem too fiercely triumphant, it makes that piece of music *more exciting*. There is now a 'London sound', owing nothing to the traditional Central European sound, taken to America by a number of trainer-conductors. And, where before I was often half-asleep, this 'London sound' makes me sit up—shaken and exultant.

2

Late on Wednesday afternoon, to my great relief Jacquetta was back from the Everglades. Wondering what I had missed—and knowing that her visual impressions and memories are much sharper than mine—I demanded an instant account of her trip down there.

'The birds were the best part,' she began, 'although of course there weren't anything like the number there would be in the winter. It's the big waders that are special—all of them beautiful, some of them rare. I saw white ibis, egrets large and small, but by far the loveliest and the rarest is the roseate spoonbill, its delicious ice-cream colour conspicious among all the snowy white birds.'

'In a way,' she continued, 'the Everglades country is rather dreary. The glades proper are olive-green expanses of saw grass with fresh water flowing slowly through them, almost invisible. Then there are great mangrove swamps broken by creeks and sea inlets. The National Park people provided me with an immensely powerful launch and a warden to drive it. We tore through these waterways at thirty knots, occasionally reining up on our haunches, as it were, to see any wild creature not already driven away by our din. Then there are the pine-lands where the ground is drier. There I saw a strange sight that made me think of a Delvaux painting—a scatter of these straight spare pines and in each one an American eagle sitting absolutely still—waiting, it might be, for the end of the world. The best times were the early mornings and the hour round about sunset. From the restaurant, where the food was quite awful, I looked over the Bay of Florida. There were spits of land, little green islets, and smooth powdery-blue water. Then against the dark clouds on the horizon huge flocks of ibis, flying in long lines, flashed in and out of the last sunlight—very far away. That was marvellous.'

I felt I had been to the Everglades and was now back in Daytona, ready for the night's concert, all in a couple of minutes.

3

The night's concert was being given by the L.S.O. Chamber
Players, its five items being performed by varied ensembles of
wind players. I was looking forward to hearing the full
orchestra again and so attended this concert dutifully rather
than eagerly, never having much enjoyed chamber music
performed entirely by brass and woodwind. This would, I
thought, be a rather boring evening. And I was wrong.
Unlike so many people now in this world of politicians,
editors, propagandists and experts, I am often wrong. It was a
delightful concert and I wish I had a recording of it.

We had two conductors. The first part was directed by
Gervase de Peyer, who knew his business but appeared to have
joined what we might call the Bernstein Ballet school of
conducting. The second was under Geoffrey Gilbert, restrained and earnest, rather like a headmaster taking a senior
class in trigonometry. The opening work, Gabriel's *Sonata
pian'e forte*, for pairs of trumpets, horns, trombones, and the
tuba, was fascinating because the players were divided into two
groups, facing each other and widely separated, so that their
sound seemed to be stereophonic. And what a grave and noble
sound good brass players produce, like so many senators in
solemn debate—but not, I think, American senators! This was
followed by Mozart's Serenade No. 12 for woodwind and
horns, and although it was well played it seemed rather tame
after the sonorous questions-and-answers of the Gabriel. After
the intermission, Gounod's *Petite Symphonie*, also for woodwind and horns, was charming, and the final item, Strauss's
one-movement serenade in E Flat, for woodwind, four horns
and the tuba, was more than charming, having moments of
real beauty. But the most rapturously received piece of the
whole evening was the quintet, for two trumpets, horn,

107]

trombone and tuba, by our own Malcolm Arnold—and not, as two separate programmes told us, 'by Matthew Arnold'. He was a good poet but no writer for the tuba, which has enormous demands made upon it by this quintet, almost turning it into a romantic instrument. And if it was anybody's evening, then it was Alan Jenkins's—fortunately for the L.S.O. a robust character. Not only had he to grapple with his tuba, he had also to grapple with the orchestra's finances, all the pay and subsistence money for a hundred men, plus wives and children, three thousand miles from home. And there were certain times at Daytona Beach, I believe, when both these responsibilities could be sharply described as being no joke.

4

I had a fresh glimpse or two of L.S.O. domestic life the following afternoon, when Jacquetta wanted to take some photographs at the Bellair Apartments. This, an enormous three-sided block at the northern edge of the town, was where many of the L.S.O. men with families rented furnished apartments. These were smallish and short of utensils, but not too bad for a month in a warm climate; they didn't overlook the beach but they were not far from it and had an adequate swimming pool of their own, where the children frolicked and their mothers came out of the water to sit and keep an eye on them and to gossip. An apartment here might cost anything up to three hundred dollars for the month; the plane fares of wives and children had to be paid for and these had gone up since the first visit; and a man with little or nothing in the bank couldn't be blamed if he decided to leave his wife and children behind or—as a few did—reluctantly refused to accept the engagement at all. (And the players, though regular members of the orchestra, are not engaged on a salary basis but instead are paid fees for each rehearsal and performance, this giving them the tax status of self-employed Schedule D men.) And no doubt many of the husbands and wives who helped their children up the steps of the chartered planes all-aboard-for-Florida knew they would have to do without this, forget about that, during the coming months, to meet their Daytona Beach expenses.

For the wives this Florida engagement had a three-fold attraction. There would be sun and sand, beach and swimming pool, for the children, who would return to face our autumnal rains looking like ripe berries. For themselves there would be sun and swimming, mornings and afternoons of lolling around without much on and talking to other wives they hardly ever met at home, and, if a baby-sitter could be found, then music and parties at night. Finally—and this was something most of them mentioned—they would be able to spend some time at last with their husbands. At home they felt they hardly saw their men, who might be off early, leaving some distant suburb, for a rehearsal or a recording, then returning late after a performance, or be away altogether on tour. (And the L.S.O. have done some lengthy tours.) A high proportion of the wives out here are musicians themselves, having met their future husbands as fellow students at the Royal Academy or the Royal College, or later playing in the same orchestra. If a scratch and perhaps jazzy band of L.S.O. wives could have given us a performance—and I think it ought to have done— it would have had, to my certain knowledge, an organist, a professional singer and two professional pianists, a harpist, several violinists, two violas, two 'cellos, a double-bass, a couple of oboes and clarinets, and its own composer, Madeleine Lord. What with babies, cleaning, cooking, shopping, probably most of these wives are out of practice, but they do at least understand the kind of life an orchestral player has to lead, a life from which these Daytona weeks are a sun-burned, salt-washed break.

It may have been the holiday air and having husbands and children within call, satisfying an atavistic desire in most normal women, that gave these L.S.O. wives a kind of bloom out there. And I am not suggesting that in London and the Home Counties they may be a pack of sullen whey-faced drabs; for all I know they may be just as attractive here too. But certainly in Daytona I was among their most constant admirers, and even now, when that beach with all its motorcars is like something half-remembered from a dream, there remains with me a lingering tendresse for all those smiling wives. If they were ever angry or sulky, it must have been early in the morning or very late at night in the seclusion of their apartments. On the beach or round the pool, wearing next to nothing, or at the concerts and the parties, all dressed up, they were equally appealing. And it is a fact that during the first week or so, whenever I happened to notice a particularly attractive woman, then almost always I found out later she was one of the L.S.O. wives. And it was not simply their faces and figures I admired. I liked their gay bearing at parties threatened by a smog of boredom; I liked their close attention to the music, especially noticeable when it was chamber music and they could be discovered among the empty seats; I liked their manner, never too playful, never too stiff; and on a deeper level of appreciation I liked the way most of them carried themselves, smiling above hidden responsibilities, worries, anxieties, with a gallant air that was both splendid and rather touching. Ladies of the L.S.O.—a portly figure, now thinning out and almost vanishing in the misty background of your Florida memories, begs to salute you!

5

During the Tenth Orchestral Concert, we were addressed by
the President of the Festival, Tippen Davidson, looking for
once unhaunted and free for a minute or two from long-
distance telephone calls. He announced that there would be
another Festival with the L.S.O. next year, and even added—
a good touch, this—that it would begin on next year's 18th
July. This announcement, I must say, was received with what
seemed to me genuine enthusiasm, bursting into shouts and
the warmest applause. The people who care about music here
may be like a speck of an island in an ocean of golfing, bridge-
playing, television-watching, but these people really *do* care,
coming to as many concerts as they can afford, and are not
tepidly flirting with culture. However, I couldn't help feeling
all over again that such people should be joined and reinforced
at the box office by others coming here from all over the place
for a musical holiday. What this Festival needs is an advance-
agent visiting every city in the Southern States. Somebody
once told me that the biggest American circuses on the road
used to employ three advance-agents, each with a different
message and manner. The first, a fairly calm and dignified
type, said in effect, 'I think I can promise you that in spite of
the extraordinary demands made upon it, the circus will be
here for a day or two.' The second, a more excitable type,
would arrive a few weeks later crying, 'Great news for you!
The date's been fixed. The circus is coming.' The third man,
only a jump ahead of the big parade, would come rushing in,
lathered in sweat and almost maniacal in his excitement,
screaming, 'They're on their way—they're nearly here—get
your tickets, for God's sake, while there's just time!' I am not
suggesting that such antics have anything to do with selling a
symphony orchestra to people, even though it may be a great

symphony orchestra and they may be rather a sleepy lot of people. I do not say that if I were running the L.S.O. I would want its concerts sold in anything like this brassy though cunning fashion. But I would object, perhaps even more strongly, to appeals begging people to fill empty seats. Perhaps one fast-moving and hard-driving advance-agent would be a reasonable compromise.

Kertesz was in charge of this concert, and he began with an excellent performance of the four-movement suite by Britten—*Sea Interludes from 'Peter Grimes'*—which I enjoyed on this occasion and enjoyed all over again at the repeat performance on the following Sunday. A Dr Chappell White, chairman of the Music Department of Emory University, Atlanta, and music critic of the *Atlanta Journal*, was among us now, writing notices for the local evening paper. And the Britten delighted him, too:

> This is first-rate pictorial music, and I was impressed once more with the extraordinary tonal range and brilliance of the L.S.O. This orchestra in this hall can produce the brightest fortissimo and the clearest pianissimo I can ever remember hearing.
>
> Kertesz kept the various colors beautifully balanced, and his control of the melodic line and the musical shape made these pieces something more than mood music.

So there! And he was equally enthusiastic—indeed, even more enthusiastic—about the next item, the Stravinsky Violin Concerto played by Goldberg—*nothing less than a masterpiece*—and, as played that night, *a thoroughly fascinating musical experience*—with cheers for *Goldberg's thorough grasp of the spirit of this unique work*—and so forth, all in a rapture. And I wish I could either agree or disagree with Dr Chappell White, but the truth is that I had never heard this complicated work before, and, though I am sure Goldberg's grasp of its spirit would be thorough, I am so blankly ignorant that I am not competent to judge either the work itself or this performance of it. Muttering through a haze, I will say that at some moments it turned towards me a face of cold strange beauty,

and that at other moments it suggested a composer who disliked violin concertos and violinists too and would rather have
been writing something else.

The whole of the second half of this concert was devoted to
Dvorak's Sixth Symphony in D, written in 1880, when
Dvorak was strongly influenced by Brahms, and the first of his
four generally-accepted symphonies—a rich plumcake of a
work, though inferior to the overdone *New World* and, my own
favourite, the great D Minor, yet another masterpiece we owe
to the London Philharmonic Society. (I have stopped worrying
about the numbering of Dvorak's symphonies; I know which
record I want partly from the key but mostly from the
pictures on the sleeves.) Kertesz had already recorded this
particular symphony with the L.S.O., and, in my capacity as a
rather idle listener, I was acquainted with it. As I get older, I
think I enjoy Dvorak more and more. His very limitations and
simplicities, frowned upon by music critics and scholars,
endear him to me. His nonsense now suits my nonsense.
Instead of commanding me to observe the march of humanity,
or to read in sound the autobiography of a neurotic genius, or
to get down on my knees before dawn to worship God, he asks
me to listen to some music—enchantingly melodic and often
exquisitely modulated, with some fascinating little tricks for
the woodwind—and so I do, and then I am delighted and
grateful. Dvorak starts with one advantage over profounder
composers: it is nobody's *duty* to listen to him; he is not
offering us a cultural leg-up; we give an ear to him simply for
our own pleasure. And pleasure is harder to come by in age
than in youth, when we can take great helpings of the solemn
and the sublime because we are feeling fine anyhow and are
not tormented by stiffening limbs, gout and insomnia.

Sensibly determined not to be lyrical over everything, Dr
Chappell White, though he praised its 'stunning virtuosity',
was severely critical of this performance of Dvorak's Symphony
in D:

[114

For all its heavy scoring and its academic symphonic form, the composition is fundamentally simple and unpretentious. It lives on the charm of its melodies, many of them touched with folk-like quality. Kertesz inflated it to the point that all charm and sense of balance was lost. Even instrumental balance suffered; the strings, which in the L.S.O. can play extremely loud, managed to keep up with the brasses, but in the loud climaxes the woodwinds were hopelessly outclassed. . . .

And here, interrupting him, I must point out that this outclassing of the woodwind was chiefly due to the fact, which I noticed very early, that they were badly seated, buried behind the strings instead of being raised above them as they normally are. The stage of the Auditorium was at fault here, not Kertesz, though it could have been argued that he should have made some allowance for this bad seating. But back to Dr White, on the whole a fair man:

The result was undeniably exciting and no end impressive as a technical feat. But it was, I'm afraid, a distortion of Dvorak.

In fairness, however, it should be said that this is evidently a minority report; the audience gave Kertesz and his colleagues a prolonged standing ovation.

There are several points worth making here. The first, a minor one, is that what brought the audience out of their seats was not distorted Dvorak but the sheer spectacular effort, both in sound and sight, of the orchestra surging and blazing through the finale. (The 'cellos alone could have been entered for the Olympic Games.) Now this may or may not have involved distorting the work, inflating it so that charm and balance vanished.

A conductor seems to me guilty of inflation when he takes a not very ambitious and cheerfully companionable symphony like this of Dvorak's and gives it a hugely portentous air as if it were about to reveal the secrets of the universe. And this Kertesz did not do, neither in this performance nor in his recording. What he might not unreasonably be accused of doing, to some extent in the recording and rather more so in

115]

this Auditorium, is over-dramatizing the work, exaggerating its crescendos, raising its temperature, 'jazzing it up'. This is unforgivable—and we have all heard it done—with a great classic, a masterwork. But Dvorak's Symphony in D is not in this class at all. I have listened to it a good many times now—and my record-player is both sensitive and wonderfully sonorous—and I consider it a fine work, but not one that has been erected on hallowed ground. Treat it as Kertesz does, and certainly there is some loss in charm, in balance, in the scale of performance that Dvorak intended. We must set against this, however, an obvious gain in dramatic brilliance and excitement, a rise in the audience's temperature too. At the end of a long sleepy day, these people were galvanized and then transported by the dazzling sheen and the glare and thunder of the last two movements. Was this worth doing? I think it was—and I was there.

But on the way home and afterwards—either there was no party that night or there was and we skipped it—I couldn't help thinking, even though ready to defend Kertesz and the L.S.O., there was at least a hint of danger now in the orchestra's sheer virtuosity, possibly tempting it to concentrate on brilliantly showy performances of not quite first-rate works—saying to us in effect, 'Now listen to what we can do with this!' It ought to be a dependable carthorse, pulling a great masterpiece safely home, as well as a racehorse for ever flashing down the course. But then I remembered they were already rehearsing the Choral Symphony for Saturday night.

6

This Friday of small accidents was 4th August. Jacquetta's birthday is the 5th, and we had decided some days before to give a late buffet-supper party after Saturday night's concert. To this birthday celebration we had invited most of our Daytona hosts and hostesses and those L.S.O. members and wives we knew best. And the food and drink were to be as good as time, money and circumstances would allow. (They were, too.) This meant that Friday was one of those days of preparation that never seem quite real; you live through them rather than in and with them; they are like plants that have roots not in the ground but somewhere in the air; and almost always I am far below my best during such days. I can rise to an occasion but I wander uncertainly, feeling vaguely depressed, through preparations for an occasion. If mistakes can be made then, I am the fellow to make them.

The mere possibility of drink running out at a party—or of guests being compelled to accept a second-best choice of tipple—horrifies me, so if I am entertaining, say, fifty people, I order sufficient booze to bring a hundred-and-fifty people close to collapse. So I didn't even take into account, for this party, one curious fact—namely, that social life in Daytona Beach, unlike social life elsewhere in many parts of the U.S., was not a hard-drinking affair. What with the thirst-making climate, the excitement of the Festival, and the hospitality offered to so many hard-working musicians, these weeks might have been one gigantic booze-up, but all the evidence I had proved they weren't. (True, I never attended one of those three-in-the-morning parties the L.S.O. boys arranged for themselves.) I had seen more people obviously plastered at any single literary party during the era 1920–1939 than I had seen at a month of parties in Daytona, where indeed I had never seen *anybody* too far on the way to being stoned. Nevertheless, following my usual practice, I went early on Friday morning to the 'liquor store'—and what a brutal name that is when compared with our 'wines and spirits merchants'!—and ordered bottles and bottles of scotch, bourbon, gin, a murderously-priced *Moet et Chandon* and a superior New York champagne (to be used when people wouldn't know the difference), and cases of beer.

Not being a complete chump, I insisted upon the same 'sale or return' arrangement I always have in London, and this was accepted without any hesitation. But here, I discovered later, was where I made my first mistake of the day. Only the unopened bottles of spirits—and very few people had drunk whisky or gin—were taken back and credited to me. Beer, I was told, was outside the sale-or-return arrangement, so that I was left with cases of it on Monday, less than twenty hours before we departed. And worse still the champagne couldn't be returned, because it had been chilled, they said; and we hadn't entirely finished even the *Moet et Chandon*, though it seemed to flow freely, to say nothing of the reserve supply of N.Y. stuff. But this situation only revealed itself on Monday, and now it is still Friday.

My second mistake that morning arose from my refusal—which always turns out to be idiotic—to accept feminine advice about what I ought to do about my body. (Women know about bodies because they are *in* them, whereas we men pretend we are at least half-out of them.) I wanted to visit a shop on Atlantic Avenue that sold very cheap but quite pretty little necklaces made of highly-polished abalone shell, which my daughters and some of my nine grand-daughters might like to have. This was approved, but what was condemned at once was my decision to walk there and back, just for the exercise. It was too hot, I was told, and the shop was further away than I thought. I dismissed this nonsense; all I had to do was to cut down Old Trail, our nearest cross-street, than take an easy

[118

stroll along Atlantic Avenue; a little 'work out' would do me good. And I was wrong, of course. The shop was much further away than I had imagined it to be, and noontide and afterwards along Atlantic Avenue was devilishly hot. Moreover, on the way back, still strolling but in a mist of sweat and idle thought, I went past the Old Trail turning, on and on until I suddenly stared about me and asked myself what I thought I was doing. (This was to repeat the question, and not for the first time, I had started with immediately after our arrival at Daytona Beach.) Drenched with sweat, clutching a paper bag filled with necklaces and various trinkets, and now a damp paper bag, I tottered in to a late lunch, thoroughly exhausted—the idiot male. Then I spent the afternoon, dropping it out of my real life, stretched on the bed, sleepy when I was holding a book and unable to sleep when I put it down.

The kitchen having been already claimed by the next night's party, we had to dine out, and we crossed the river to the San Remo, to which the McLemores had taken us. In the middle of dinner I knocked over my glass, flooding the table with red wine. I was quite sober and not in a bad temper, making large angry gestures; I had simply misjudged—as I had recently done before and was to do again—the height of the glass; I am probably breaking up. Our waiter, an elderly man who was not breaking up, cut short my apologies when he came to rescue the table by pretending, in an altogether unexpected and whimsical fashion, that *he* had knocked over the glass and spilt the wine, that it was the kind of thing he was always doing, and he went on grumbling at himself, but forgiving himself, until the table was neat and white again. I had hardly noticed him when we had been ordering dinner, but now it was as if he had suddenly been transformed into one of those old waiters who had so often served us at the Krantz-Ambassador, in the Neuer Markt, Vienna. If he had gone into their endless sing-song, *Bitte schön, Danke schön*, I wouldn't have been surprised. I looked forward to having some talk with this whimsical waiter, so unAmerican, but we had to get to the concert that night, and then, through no fault of mine, as we shall see, I could never sit at his table again.

The concert, the Eleventh, took us even more directly to Austria, for Kertesz was conducting Mahler's Fourth Symphony, with Judith Raskin, from the N.Y. Met and an excellent soprano (she had already given a successful recital), at his elbow to describe the joys of Heaven in the fourth movement. And I felt when it was all over that Kertesz and Miss Raskin and the L.S.O. had been fully equal to the task, never easy, of interpreting Mahler. What remained in question was my own ability to appreciate Mahler. In spite of the efforts of my friend Cardus—and I think I can call him that, even though we rarely meet nowadays—to turn me by way of records, pamphlet-programmes, books, into a Mahler man, I still dither in ambivalence. I am far from being one of those solemn asses who deny Mahler originality and creative genius, who suggest he is giving us a lot of upsidedown *Kapell-meistermusik*. Any critic who thinks *Das Lied von der Erde* was somehow concocted out of bits of unfamiliar operas should not have an editor or a publisher but a psychiatrist. I have loved that great magical sad work for many years now. And I am ready to believe almost everything Cardus says about Mahler, and there are moments, a good many of them too, when I listen alone to the various recordings I have of Mahler and I seem to *feel* what Cardus has felt. But then there is always something I dislike, some gritty pieces of shell in the lobster mousse.

It happened all over again with this performance of the Fourth Symphony. Yes, yes, yes—so much smaller, so much simpler, so much finer (no heavy brass) in its texture, than the others—easy and a treat, you might almost say a rural school treat! But as soon as that *chirrup, chirrup, chirrup* begins, I feel a mounting irritation. The bitter neurotic introvert, the savage martinet of the Imperial Opera of Vienna, instantly rouses my prejudice when he is in this mood, as if he has put on a comic hat and is pretending to be Dvorak's uncle. Everything that belongs to childlike innocence in this symphony, from the first *chirrups* to all that singing about a holiday-camp Paradise in the last movement, I find almost unendurable. I don't want it—as Mahler thinks he does—to win. It is only when it is losing hands down, when in the second movement Death and his screeching fiddle are haunting the village green, and when the third movement forces us into a terrible melancholy and we know that childlike innocence hasn't a chance, that I can listen fascinated, entranced. There is of course—and surely it is one of the most *surprising* passages in all symphonic music, and proof enough of Mahler's originality —that sudden crescendo, in a changed key, towards the end of the third movement, when the trumpets call from high battlements, the cymbals give us one triumphant clash, the drum thumps out the movement of gigantic bolts and bars, and there is a swirling mist of strings and woodwind—and we are offered, it seems, a glimpse of Paradise opening its gates. But then, almost before we have recovered from the surprise, the gates have vanished like a dream, and we ache again from a strange homesickness. And for me that is the real end. I don't want a fourth movement that conducts me through those gates, by way of *Das Knaben Wunderhorn,* and takes me through a celestial agricultural show and holiday camp and asks me to listen to angelic voices. I don't like this false-naïve Gustav Mahler. It is the death-haunted and homesick-for-another-world Mahler who is my man. So, knowing what was coming and what I would feel about it, I ought to have crept out at the end of the third movement. Staying on was that Friday's final mistake.

7

Saturday morning's paper had a photograph of Barry Tuckwell (referred to as 'George Tuckwell' just for the hell of it) bending over a record-player and an elderly gentleman, who was shown touching the record-player in that curiously unnatural fashion which all press photographers seem to prefer. It appeared that Mr Abercrombie, aged seventy-three, had been an invalid for nearly thirty years, had never been to a live concert until two weeks before, had been fond of music all his life and had kept an L.S.O. scrapbook for these two seasons, but had no record-player that would enable him to hear 'that wonderful music' again. So the L.S.O. gave him one. This could have been a little publicity stunt—and I meant to check it, but forgot—but let us assume it wasn't and for a moment all feel a trifle better.

Fleeing from a house that looked as if it might be opening as a night club, we decided to cross the river again and lunch at the San Remo, where I hoped to renew my acquaintance with the whimsical Krantz-style waiter. We told each other the place looked very quiet for a Saturday lunchtime, and indeed it *was* very quiet—it was closed. (And I never saw that waiter again because the San Remo is closed on Mondays, and we left at dawn on Tuesday.) Now it was too late to try another neighbourhood, so we went, probably looking rather gloomy (one of us anyhow, because I have the opposite of a poker face, one that *over-expresses* my feelings, going round with me giving a ham performance), to a rather honky-tonky-style place, the Dutch Kitchen, one of a chain of popular restaurants. And within its modest limits it was quite good, far better—as I have noticed before—than a chain restaurant (as distinct from a teashop) would be in England. Americans feed well on this level; it is when they have more money and go in for

[122

gracious living and fabulous continental cuisines that they are humbugged and swindled. I remember, years ago, when I was occupying a suite in one of New York's most famous and expensive hotels, I used to sneak out and enjoy a much better breakfast, at a quarter the price, at the nearest Childs.

We were now approaching an evening—a Saturday night that really was *a Saturday Night*, which most Saturday nights aren't—that had an L.S.O. Ninth Symphony and a birthday party high on the programme. Just try to match that, musically and socially! And I should like to add that I was all eagerness, impatience, growing excitement. But the truth is I felt nothing of the sort. (I mention this because of what follows at the concert.) Two or three weeks earlier, the eagerness and excitement would have possessed me. Now I wasn't quite *in* Daytona Beach as I had been then. Half of me, you might say, was no longer there. It was hovering round an imagined Martha's Vineyard, where we were to go next to stay with friends, and wondering if the painting chances there would be better than they had been here. I no longer felt committed to this Festival. I hadn't *had it* but I had nearly had it. This was not a criticism of the Festival, the L.S.O., Daytona Beach; it was an attitude of mind arising from the depths of my nature, for I must confess I am a restless and impatient man. This may seem unlikely when I can pass weeks and weeks in the country, quietly writing, walking round the village every afternoon, seeing few people. But when I am doing this, I am not only meeting the demands of my profession but I am also assuaging my natural restlessness and impatience by chasing and trying to capture another work idea, and the sheer variety of the work tells its own tale. And as soon as the work is done and I have left home, then I want to keep on the move, never stopping anywhere long. I am a rather bad traveller, and this is mostly impatience too, but I am an eager mover-on, to whom this jet age does at least make one instant appeal, for I never catch sight of an airline itinerary—*Athens, Rome, Teheran, Karachi,*

123]

and the rest—without wanting to be off. So now I wasn't already half-out of Daytona because I disliked it but because I was anxious to get along to the next place.

For this, the Twelfth Orchestral Concert, the Auditorium was full and the platform was even fuller. Somehow and somewhere behind the orchestra the 160 members of the Atlanta Choral Guild had been packed in, and not since my teens, when I used to visit the galleries of music halls, where expert packers-in were employed, have I seen so many people crammed into so small a space. Nearly half of them must have been well behind the sound reflectors hanging above the main stage, so that it would be both absurd and unfair to offer any judgment of their singing. However, they had been carefully coached—Horenstein himself had gone up to Atlanta to take their last rehearsals—and the sound they made, beginning with Bach's Cantata No. 50, was pleasant enough, though I couldn't help thinking that fewer but more sonorous voices— say, about twenty-four choral singers from Huddersfield, Bradford or Sheffield—would have served Bach and us rather better.

A very short first half, to make room for the Ninth after the intermission, ended with the prelude to *Parsifal*, which I thought Horenstein and the L.S.O. played extremely well. Dr Chappell White—and I am glad to bring him in again—said in his notice later that while he approved of the tempo, he disapproved of the tone colour. The L.S.O., he concluded ruefully, fell 'short of Wagner's warm orchestral color'. Well, I don't wish to quarrel with Dr Chappell White, especially now when we must part, but I felt that this *Parsifal* prelude was given all the orchestral colour it demands, which, in my genuinely humble opinion, is not a great amount. This is no Brahms's Third Symphony, all warmly autumnal, and I would say it asks for a kind of white intensity rather than much splashing of colour. I have listened to this prelude many times, mostly, I must admit, in various recordings I have. And I

[124

never hear it without remembering our old friend, Violet Hammersley, a famous musical hostess in her time. When she stayed with us here in Alveston, she was well into her eighties, frail and rather deaf, and she would lie on the sofa in my study and command me to put on a recording of this prelude, with the sound turned nearly full up, and would insist upon hearing it over and over again, entranced by those piercing tones that threatened to bring all the books off their shelves. When she was beginning to forget so much, she remembered that *Parsifal* prelude in her letter of thanks; and we never saw her again for not long afterwards she died.

Now—alas for me—the Ninth Symphony! And back to Dr Chappell White—it is his final appearance—who is rapturous:

> In the first movement, Horenstein took a conservative tempo, emphasizing the monumental character with little sacrifice of the excitement. The impeccable clarity of the L.S.O. made the Scherzo a major achievement, and the slow movement was, as Beethoven must have intended, a vision of pure beauty. . . .

Then there are three paragraphs, judicial but sympathetic, about the singing that we can pass over to hurry towards his enthusiastic conclusion:

> But the final word of praise must go to Jascha Horenstein and the L.S.O.—and as always to Beethoven. The Ninth Symphony remains one of the great uplifting experiences, and one always has a special feeling of gratitude for the opportunity of hearing it. The capacity audience expressed its gratitude on this occasion by a spontaneous, immediate standing ovation.

And bravo for Dr Chappell White! I agree most warmly with everything he says. But now I can only hope that what follows will never catch his eye. No sooner were we launched into the fourth movement than I began to feel bored. For the first time out of many, this great uplifting experience was eluding me. The closer we came to universal brotherhood, with everybody and everything on the platform pounding away, the harder I wished it was all over. By the time Schiller, Beethoven and the Atlanta Choral Guild were ready to embrace millions and had a kiss for all the world, I had one foot beating impatiently in the aisle, longing to be off. Probably I leapt up—if I can leap up—with everybody else for the standing ovation, but I was moved not by gratitude and joy but by a feeling of sheer relief.

True, I had always heard the Choral Symphony better sung, both by its quartet and its chorus, though these people really weren't bad. But Horenstein and the L.S.O. had been in magnificent form. And so of course had Beethoven. I was at fault, not any of them. For various reasons, vague but probably faintly disreputable, I just didn't want a great uplifting experience, and recoiled into boredom or irritation when Beethoven and his performers insisted upon trying to hammer me into one. I reacted just as sharply against Beethoven's determined sublimity as I had done against Tschaikowsky's insistent pathos. The time had been—and it would only return in a fifth dimension—when I had been shaken and then raised to glory by this giant of a symphony. It is when we are young that we best discover glorious news in the sublime, a wonderful reply to all our eager expectations; and this is why every effort should be made to offer youth the noblest works of art. When we are into our seventies—or at least this is my experience—we can be more enravished and moved by a brief passage—a distant horn call, woodwind bubbling and fading, the sudden lament of a single violin or 'cello—than by a whole gigantic, thundering finale. We can be enticed but not summoned and drummed into the brotherhood of Man. One voice with the right cadence might do it, but we harden ourselves against two-hundred-and-fifty determined performers. And of course Beethoven can do it; he has been doing it to me—though lately more in moments than in hours—for at least sixty years.

Was the birthday party a success? I can never answer this when one of our own parties is in question. It *seemed* to go very well; that is the best I can do. We were lucky, for once, with our Daytona house, for not only was the sitting-room fairly

[126

large but it was also L-shaped. This meant that people could go on talking in one part of the room while in the other we could play a few games, which we were determined to do after so many parties where the people talked to one another, night after night. And I am glad to report that in this game-playing our closest allies were my favourites, the L.S.O. wives. But throughout the evening our most valuable ally was a young man called, let us say, Johnson. I had asked our neighbour and friend, Henry McLemore, if he thought I might be able to find a man who could act as a drinks waiter for us. He said I could leave it to him, and then announced later that for fifteen dollars Johnson would be our man. Where Henry found Johnson I was never able to discover, but never were fifteen dollars better spent in Daytona Beach. Johnson was the exact opposite of all the disillusioned sub-butlers and weary elderly wine waiters who come round with the drinks at so many London parties, usually arriving with fewer and fewer at longer and longer intervals, and often contriving to suggest it is time you stopped hanging around for free booze and went home. Johnson had a wide grin and a breezy manner, was young, quick and tireless, and instead of being *against* the party, like so many of those old frauds in London, he was not only all *for* it but identified himself with it so completely that somehow he *was* the party, the hospitable social substance compared with which Jacquetta and I were mere shadows. He made me feel—and quite without resentment, let me add— that at any moment he might not only join in the games but easily win all the prizes. And if he didn't do this, that was because he noticed—and he was a quick noticer—that some people needed a few more drinks. When he asked me, as he did whenever we were face to face, 'How's it going?' winking and twinkling, he was really asking me how I felt at that particular moment, wondering without anxiety if I was still on the up-and-up. He wasn't asking how the party was going: he *was* the party. And I can't send him a copy of this book because we

127]

never had his address. Perhaps he hadn't an address. Perhaps he was a being—known in some parts of the East Indies as a *tulpa*—created for that evening by the McLemores and ourselves out of our combined thoughts, feelings, wishes. It is almost as easy for me to believe this now as it is for me to believe that Daytona Beach still exists somewhere.

8

When I was a small boy and my parents asked me what I had been doing, four times out of five I replied, 'Nothing.' And that is what I was doing during most of that last Sunday in Daytona. However, in the early evening we did attend a cocktail party of sorts, and I remember it because it produced the only really unpleasant encounter of our month's stay. (A tribute this to Florida manners and good humour. Could an American stay four weeks here in England, meeting scores and scores of people, and then remember only *one* unpleasant encounter?) I learnt afterwards that this bulky spectacled man prided himself on his bluntness and was sharply anti-British. He came up at once with two nasty loaded questions, and I answered the first one politely, but when the second one arrived I had had enough, and staring hard at him I said that if he was trying to be offensive he was doing quite well; after which we avoided each other. Just two or three minutes, that is all, out of at least a hundred hours of pleasant discourse! They might have been less pleasant if those who favoured the war in Vietnam, probably a majority, hadn't always taken care never to mention it, whereas those who shared our own view spoke out quite openly. It is a fact—and one for which I can claim no credit, being ready to argue almost anywhere at any time—that never once did I find myself in some noisy debate about Vietnam. There may have been among these Daytonans an unformulated rule, an unspoken agreement, about being polite and indeed friendly towards their London visitors, and only this one bulky, blunty, anti-British type went his own unsweet way, but, if he didn't want to get clobbered, did at least choose as a possible victim someone equally bulky, blunty, and very firmly anti-anti-Britishy.

The Sunday orchestral concerts had always been repeats of

Thursday's, but on this last night the exact pattern was broken. The Britten *Sea Interludes* and the Dvorak Sixth Symphony were being given again, but in the place of Goldberg's performance of the Stravinsky Violin Concerto we had Ashkenazy playing Mozart's Piano Concerto in B Flat, K.595. There was this other difference too, that here was the very last night, the end of 1967's Festival. The Auditorium was full, and I think all the enthusiasts must have been there: the place was charged with feeling. The Britten pieces came and went, just as well played—and under Kertesz too, of course—as they had been on Thursday. And at last some Mozart, with the Piano Concerto, came exquisitely to life. Bent over the keyboard like a visitant elf, Ashkenazy gave us a beautiful performance. In the middle movement, the Larghetto, the piano ceased to be a percussive instrument; very quietly, very delicately, he made it sing; this was no longer an elf but some other kind of being, humming to himself as he wandered across Elysian fields. The concert ended once more with the Dvorak, and Kertesz, ignoring Dr Chappell White, kept right on 'distorting' the composer and the work, with the climaxes all blazing and thundering away at us, making us marvel at this final proof of the orchestra's energy and vitality. What—after so much sun and bathing and sandcastles for the kids and 'shrimp boils' and hot-dogs-and-softball afternoons and late-night parties and mornings of rehearsal and evenings of performing—all this—and after packing to make an early start for tomorrow's planes! It was incredible, and as if to prove it was even further from credibility the audience refused to let the orchestra leave the platform and demanded and received two encores and would not disperse until the two national anthems ordered them to stand still and then to go. Some of these people wept; all seemed to be moved; and even I, already half-gone from Daytona and wanting to be wholly gone, preferring to listen to the L.S.O. where it rightly belonged—in London, felt some stirring and prickling of emotion. And after all this the

[130

reception-party at the Yacht Club, a final gesture of Daytona goodwill, was rather an anti-climax. I saw many of the musicians there, and if I didn't thank them for all those evenings of glorious sound, then I ought to have done—and do so now.

9

Monday morning, 7th August, was departure time for all London visitors except Jacquetta and me. For some reason I cannot discover now we had decided from the first to stay until Tuesday, and a complicated series of plane bookings, from Daytona to Martha's Vineyard, Mass., made it almost impossible for us to change our minds without going right out of them. A friendly neighbour, who had never been to Cape Kennedy herself, was ready to take Jacquetta there, so she was off for the day. But before she went, I had already been called for, at about 7.30, to broadcast in somebody's daily Breakfast Hour. This served me right. After all these years I still believe that if I put off something I don't want to do, not sensibly refusing it but postponing it, then it may never happen. On the very first night of the Festival, at that Gala affair, a vivacious but obstinate blonde had collared me, insisting that I must do a broadcast—apparently a great treat for all concerned—on her breakfast programme. And instead of saying No, like a man, I weakly consented but did my usual putting-it-off trick, forgetting that it hardly ever works. So there I was, beginning this last day in Daytona by sitting in a booth in a restaurant with this ruthless lady and a microphone, at eight in the morning, breakfastless on a solid hour's breakfast programme.

Once we were on the air, my companion's vivacity bubbled and boiled. 'And a very *very good* goodmorning it is!' I seem to remember her declaring to the listeners. She was more enthusiastic about everything than I have ever been about anything. I said to her afterwards, 'When you describe so many people as wonderful, *wonderful* persons, what do you say if you really like somebody?' But I hadn't to spend most of the hour grunting replies to her questions, which were harmless enough,

[132

never loaded; she must have passed about half the hour making ecstatic references to various products and merchandise that were subsidizing the local network, her and the programme, in fact everybody on the job there—*except me*. And here I ask to make an announcement, the real reason for mentioning this broadcast at all. Over thirty-five years or so, in one part of America and another, I must have given scores and scores, possibly hundreds, of broadcasts—and really *given* them because I have never been paid a cent. The radio was commercial but I wasn't. Now if everybody is doing it for nothing, I won't expect a fee. (And this can happen with small educational radio and television stations—and good luck to them!) But I hereby announce that Daytona, if it chose to listen at breakfast time on 7th August 1967, caught my final appearance on commercial radio as an unpaid broadcaster. After over thirty-five years of it—now, as I once heard a man say, 'Limit reached!'

There were two charter flights for the L.S.O. and its dependants and impedimenta. The smaller plane left for New York from Daytona Airport. The larger plane went from the bigger airport at Orlando, sixty or seventy miles away. And the departure for Orlando (and there's a Shakespearean destination for you!), whether by buses or private cars, set out from the Daytona Plaza Hotel, to which I made my way about the middle of the morning. The area round the entrance and the lobby beyond suggested the immediate possibility of a small revolution, perhaps the minor keys revolting against the major keys, or the outbreak of a little war between sharps and flats. All was confusion and baggage and a sorting out of families and packages. Wives kept running back to find something they missed. Children suddenly appeared with all those unsuitable things they will never leave behind. Gigantic buses, as heavy and thick-sided as battle cruisers, were either groaningly departing or coming up, shivering and roaring. There were greetings and farewells, distressed maidens

133]

reluctantly releasing young violinists, and tears and smiles and shouts and wavings.

When her particular group had gone, a girl I didn't know, probably a student, said to me, 'Oh—but the stamina and vitality of these men! Gosh, they're amazing!' I told her that we are rather a lazy and careless people but, whatever we may pretend, still a fairly tough people. But I wasn't feeling tough at that moment. Though I had no reason for feeling sad, though I was really only waiting to get out of the place myself, such is empathy that I felt sad. The boys and the music had gone; brightness had fallen from the air; the trumpets were going back over the sea.

About nineteen hours later, the most intelligent girl in our neighbourhood rose far too early, and, under a dawn that might have been borrowed from the Indian Ocean, drove us to Daytona Airport. On the plane to Atlanta we saw Florida fall away from us and turn into a mere blur, and we ate one of those cardboard breakfasts. At Atlanta Airport, which seems to have the longest of all corridors, we were given another ride in a little electric car from gate to gate. At Kennedy Airport, N.Y., we found ourselves in some strange outlying region of domestic air transport, then walked to one more farflung still, where a plane to Martha's Vineyard, Mass., might be discovered— though it wouldn't be if there was fog over the island, as there is all too often. And while we waited, Jacquetta vanished to order a bowl of soup somewhere; and I had a drink and then bought several magazines that I took to the island but never read. (In airports I behave like a sailor home from the sea, buying anything.) There was no fog reported; the plane went; and by early afternoon we were down on Martha's Vineyard, where we were met by our friend Evelyn Ames (a good writer), with whom we were staying.

'I lived near there,' she said, referring to Daytona Beach, 'for some time during the war. And I can't imagine what you'll make of it.'

[134

'Neither can I,' was the only reply I could give her. And I meant it too, for at that moment, only about ten hours away from our last glimpse of Crescent Ridge Road, Halifax Drive, Atlantic Avenue, and the rest, the Florida International Music Festival and Daytona Beach had splintered and then dissolved into bewildering dream fragments: not a good dream, not a bad dream, but odd and strange—a bit off and rum and peculiar in all its aspects—as so many dreams are. Would I ever be able to turn these wispy dream fragments into solid jigsaw pieces and then fit them together without even a picture to guide me?

I didn't know then. I don't know now.

Finale

tema con varazione—tutti

'I know there are people who say that the symphony orchestra is dead.' I have taken this from an interview in *The Times* today with Bernard Haitink, who is the conductor of the Concertgebouw and of course does not believe that the symphony orchestra is dead. How could he when he has just agreed to conduct yet another symphony orchestra as well as the Concertgebouw? He is not a vampire wanting to feed on corpse after corpse. But who are these people who say that the symphony orchestra is dead? They are the farthest-out and most militant members of the *avant garde*.

They are more or less the same people who tell us that painting not abstract or Pop or Op is dead, that drama that is not simply a 'happening' is dead, that the novel in any recognizable shape is dead, and that those of us, a gigantic majority, who are not far out with them in the movement are probably dead too. No doubt a few of these people, a minority of a minority, are genuine revolutionary artists—for example, composers who cannot think in terms of a conventional orchestra and really want four pianos, brass and percussion sections, and five tape-recorders. They may also want, perhaps without being consciously aware of it, to hasten the process of disintegration in our society and to ally themselves with various de-personalizing, de-humanizing factors already at work in it. Apart from these very few, the rest of these 'Now you're dead' people are just so many fashionable sillies, all the happier being so trendy because way out there, in the van, nothing need be taken too seriously or be the object of careful study. After all, it's

[136

fun to be so advanced that Aunt Edna and old Uncle Charles can hardly see you. It is worth adding that this cry 'Oh—it's dead now' comes at a time when the glossy, modish, model-haunted magazines handle the arts as if they were skirts and hats, coming 'in' and going 'out' every season. This means that the *avant garde* will have to keep running hard to avoid being called old-fashioned—in fact, dead. And those of us who were dead years ago, who are now enjoying a fairly cosy after-life, will be able to observe these desperate runners with some amusement.

For something that is dead the symphony orchestra is behaving very strangely. It insists upon reproducing itself, and not only in Western Europe and America but also in parts of the world, for example the Far East, where until recently it was almost unknown. And on summer evenings the parks in America and the 'Proms' in London are packed with people, most of them young and lively, who do not seem to realize they are attending the funeral services of the symphony orchestra. There are also all the recordings, more and more and more of them made by ghosts, now to be bought in every High Street or Main Street. And the television and radio programme planners, who give so much time to symphonic music, seem to be incapable of realizing that they are trafficking with the dead. Even *The Times* leader-writers note the astonishing activity of these ghosts, for one wrote the other day:

> The musician, surveying mankind a little more extensively than Dr Johnson, from Tokyo to Peru, is startled by the world-wide spread of western music. The Far East contributes players and conductors to the west, and the work of singers, instrumentalists and conductors who have never travelled east of Budapest is eagerly heard and discussed in Alice Springs or Osaka. . . .

And now that is enough of this *dead* nonsense. The symphony orchestra is gigantically and astoundingly alive. And without reducing a single town to ruins, without slicing off an arm or leg anywhere, it has now conquered the world. It has done it not by munitions but by magic.

For a long time now I have believed that the symphony orchestra is one of the greatest achievements of Western Man. Perhaps it is his noblest achievement. And this is true of the symphony orchestra at all its stages of development, from the modest ensembles of the Eighteenth Century to the huge complicated orchestras demanded by the late nineteenth-century composers—quadruple woodwind, eight horns, five trumpets, and the rest. (The dinners of their patrons were on the same scale, which was, we might say, Imperial.) Since Strauss and Mahler piled up their instrumentalists, row upon row, there has been a marked tendency to reduce the orchestra to a more manageable size, the result at first of a different style of composition, thinner and wirier, less elaborate in its orchestration, and perhaps, more recently still, another result of the increasing costs of rehearsals and performances by large orchestras. A modern composer may not want to write for four pianos, brass and percussion sections, and five tape-recorders, may love the sound of a full symphony orchestra, but may also have to remind himself that the services of such an orchestra, if it has a high reputation, can cost a concert promoter about £2,000. (It was probably about £200 when the L.S.O. gave its first concert, in the summer of 1904.) Yes, the price is high. But then it usually is high now for severely-disciplined skills, and a fine symphony orchestra, with perhaps 90 men playing like one extraordinary sensitive monster with 180 arms, is a marvellous assembly of such skills. We are always being asked now to wonder at the 'miracle' of this and that, and we forget that we have been living alongside a continuing miracle all our lives—that of any great symphony orchestra.

As we approach old age we are less susceptible and less responsive than we used to be—and this will have been evident to younger readers of the foregoing chapters here—but in my time I have been shaken to my depths and then lifted to ecstatic heights by almost the mere *sound* of a large

[138

orchestra. I can never forget a few moments early in 1919. I had spent four-and-a-half years in the army, and during all that time I had heard nothing but scratchy records, what passed for music at camp entertainments, and a few bands accompanying variety shows. I was starved of noble sound. Then at last I attended a concert again, my first real concert since the summer of 1914, and there came to my ears, rising like the tide of some magic sea, the sound of a large-scale orchestra. It was so overwhelming that I had to summon every resource of the will to keep silent and reasonably still; I wanted to laugh aloud, to bang about and wave my arms, to behave in fact exactly as I once saw and heard, years before, a lunatic behave in the side gallery of a concert. During those first moments, I was that wild man merely with the lid still on. But inside, where I really lived, the lid was off. The inner me was laughing aloud, banging about, waving arms, suddenly bewitched.

I will admit that during those four weeks in Daytona Beach I attended more concerts than I do in a year now, here at home. This is chiefly because for the most part either I am here in the country, working hard, or I am abroad somewhere, enjoying a painting holiday, and into the few days a month I spend in London—unless I have gone up with some special concert in mind—I cram so many engagements that I have no time left for the Royal Festival Hall. (And I have to be dragged, protesting, to the Albert Hall.) And so, like many elderly former concert-goers, I take most of my music from recordings and a record-player, which, as I have already suggested, is an exceptionally good one, built for me by an acoustic engineer. Now I am not saying that this is an entirely satisfactory substitute for live performances. (Though I will say that some musical persons exaggerate the defects of recordings and have probably never heard them at their best.) For example, the familiar practice in recording of perfecting one short passage before moving on to the next makes for a loss of continuity and sweep; then, however good the record and the record-player, there is a certain loss of scale (even more obvious in performances coming over the air, by way of sound engineers who turn up a solitary oboe or flute and then turn down a *fortissimo* by the full orchestra); and there is a lack of the excitement that comes through the eye as well as the ear, and of any sense of occasion, and of all the feeling created by the presence of 2,000 other people who are also listening.

Even so, with good recordings and record-players that are both sensitive and sonorous, it is possible now to distinguish between a really first-rate symphony orchestra, a glorious ensemble, and one that is merely painstaking and adequate. A great orchestra can now establish its greatness ten thousand miles away from its usual concert hall. It may rehearse and perform in London, Vienna or Cleveland, Ohio, yet enravish listeners who have never set eyes on these cities, who live in Bengal, Queensland or Kenya. Therefore—and this is the point I have been approaching so laboriously—it is far more important today than it ever was before, when no orchestra had a world audience, that great symphony orchestras with a style and character of their own should exist, should be maintained, and should never be allowed to fall below their highest standard. And while this is easy to write, it is appallingly difficult to bring into actual practice. Keeping an orchestra on a very high level is like playing croquet in Alice's Wonderland. It presents some knotty problems. And I passed part of my time at Daytona Beach examining some of the knots.

2

Like André Previn, I am ready to declare that the L.S.O. as it is today is my favourite orchestra. For a long time it wasn't, indeed it wasn't even in the running; the next few years may see it begin to go down again; and this uncertainty will be gnawing away to the end of my *Finale*. But at the present time I would rather hear the L.S.O. play any major work it knows and identifies itself with than listen to any other orchestra anywhere playing the same work. I am not declaring that the L.S.O. is superior to any other orchestra in every respect. That would be silly. Could any orchestra of this century ever have made a reasonable claim to all-round superiority? No, not a reasonable one. I remember a new orchestra for which such a claim was being made—by radio publicity men. It was certainly the most *expensive* symphony orchestra ever assembled. I am going back thirty years now to the time when N.B.C. in New York, having Toscanini under contract to do a series of broadcasts, provided the maestro with a de-luxe orchestra, in which almost every section contained several principals from other American orchestras. Strads were as common as resin, and possibly the brass was all pure gold. I was offered the privilege—though now I can't imagine why—of listening to this N.B.C. orchestra, not over the air but sitting in the same studio. Yet even under Toscanini, still only seventy then, this orchestra completely failed to suggest any all-round superiority; in fact it seemed to me disappointingly characterless; it was a lot of money and had no soul.

There may be orchestras—though not here in Britain—more exactly disciplined and powerfully welded together than the L.S.O. There may be others that continually produce a richer and mellower sound, equally pleasing to Viennese and American ears, in concerts offering lashings of chocolate and whipped cream. It is a fact—and anybody not aware of it has not been reading this book but skipping through it—that the open and vibratory tone of the L.S.O. woodwind can seem an offence across the Atlantic; and even its strings, as they rise so fiercely to a climax, can be regarded over there with disapproval. I will admit all this and more, yet still declare the L.S.O. my favourite. I will also admit that personal prejudice may be hard at work here: its nonsense may suit my nonsense.

Any prejudice I may have in favour of this orchestra goes back a long way, to the years, which I cherish, before the First War, when my friends were still alive and twentieth-century Man was not yet a blood-soaked lunatic. I had been brought up symphonically on the Hallé—a very solid orchestra, playing under the even solider Hans Richter the solidest German masterworks. Then one night some strangers arrived and at once changed the whole atmosphere of St George's Hall, Bradford, charging it with electricity and apparently filling it with colour from the palest purest blue to menacing clouds of indigo and violet sheets of lightning. These sorcerers from the South, for whom nobody had prepared me, were the L.S.O. conducted by Nikisch. (This was the L.S.O. too which, perhaps through the influence of his friend W. H. Reed, did so much for Elgar.) And though that susceptible youth is about fifty-five years behind me, though I am fat and gouty and would not consent to sit on a wooden bench for two hours even to hear a choir of angels, the L.S.O. as it is today, after a long darkish interval, can create in me, as no other orchestra can, *something of that old excitement*. And although that may not sound much—I don't know what goes on inside you—as far as I am concerned, it is saying a hell of a lot.

As Previn suggested, the L.S.O. today is at once elegant and exciting. It offers us both delicacy and fire. It owes its elegance, its delicacy, largely to the exceptional virtuosity of its principals, technically masters of their instruments but also good musicians.

These men may be said to have added another dimension to orchestral playing. They belong to what the N.B.C. ought to have been but wasn't. I am not saying that they are altogether superior to the best of the old orchestral principals, who may have retired to teach them, but whereas the older exceptional players were scattered, these L.S.O. men are all performing at the same time and are still comparatively young. And this takes us from the elegance to the excitement. As far as its actual playing members are concerned, the L.S.O. is now a young orchestra and, with an average age somewhere in the earlier thirties, must be the youngest of all the world's great orchestras. (Seeing some of these on television, which offers us at least a good look if not a good listen, I couldn't help noticing their heavy middle-age appearance. No tender-hearted Daytona girls would have wept in *those* arms.) A fair number of these L.S.O. men must still be in their twenties, as indeed I know some of them are. The youngest of all, a 'cellist, Christopher Green, is only twenty-one; at sixteen he won a scholarship to the Royal College and worked under Pini, spent some months in Paris with Tortelier, and had a year with the London Philharmonic before joining the L.S.O.; and I suggest we bear him in mind as an example of a recruit. It is he and his sort who add excitement to the elegance, fire to the delicacy.

It is not only that these comparative newcomers have youth, enthusiasm, vitality, they have also an attitude of mind, a way of thinking about themselves, that only a very few of the old orchesrtal players had. I believe they regard themselves primarily as musicians, not as instrumentalists. They are not holding down a job but are making music. So rehearsals are personally important to them. Their pride is involved in a fine performance. With superb principals either to give them a lead or hold them together; with a conductor they respect but are not afraid of (a subject to which we will return); they can risk feeling excited themselves and are able to communicate this excitement. So when, after playing with infinite delicacy, this

143]

orchestra has to let go, it lets go. And—letting go, myself—this is for me, man!

This new type of orchestral player may want to have a giggle or two at a dullish rehearsal or as a momentary relief from strained concentration, but unlike many of the old instrumentalists, often boozy military-band men, neither during rehearsal nor at a performance is he looking at his watch and wondering when he can down his next pint. He is not stolidly blowing away for a living; he wants a living—and a good living—but he also wants to be making music. Such music, however, has a broad base; it is not confined within the limits of symphonic orchestral work; it may take him into some chamber ensemble, a jazz group, or an orchestra of sorts improvised to record film music. But this, you may say, is simply the familiar frantic run-around and scramble for fees against which the older orchestral players, longing for security and a reasonable amount of leisure, were always protesting. So it would seem. However, the wheel, so often moving towards irony, has turned almost a full circle. When regular salaries and security might soon be had for the asking, many of these young musicians don't want them. And—a final irony—they are encouraged by their directors, whom they elect, not to want them. A situation I was well acquainted with twenty-five years ago has now been almost entirely reversed. This was one of the surprises, perhaps the most impressive of them, that came springing out of the talk I had at Daytona Beach.

This talk was always on an easy social level, over coffee at a rehearsal break or drinks and spiced ham at one of the parties. I never had any intention of going round with a set of questions and a notebook. I never in fact sought out, for deliberate opinion-sampling, any particular member or director of the orchestra. And because the talk was social and more or less confidential, no names will be attached to it here, though in most instances I could easily supply them. If a certain vagueness creeps in, that cannot be helped. On the other hand,

[144

the men I talked to told me what they really felt and not what they might be expected to feel.

Over and over again, baiting the hook, I would ask in effect if the time hadn't come when London should have at least one great symphony orchestra—and clearly the L.S.O. was indicated—that would be raised high above this scurrying round for a fee here and a fee there. The members of this soundly-established permanent orchestra, like so many on the Continent and in America, would be paid ample regular salaries, would not be overworked, could enjoy proper holidays and look forward to a decent pension. In return they would devote themselves entirely to the orchestra and would be forbidden to accept any work outside it. And there were some L.S.O. men who agreed with this, out of a belief that only in this way could an orchestra with a high standard be maintained. But many more disagreed. And it was not a question of money. They declared that the extra work, away from the orchestra—film work, for example—broke the routine, added variety and zest. They played better for the orchestra just because they were not always with it. Even if they had more time for rehearsal—and I pointed out that they would have, especially if, like most of the great Continental and American permanent orchestras, they repeated their programmes—they said they would always be in danger of becoming dull, giving routine performances, turning into civil service musicians. It seemed as if the very qualities of character and mind that made their best performances so exciting—and this of course has been acknowledged—protested against any plan to give their work permanence and security. So what so many older English instrumentalists had dreamt of, had wistfully described in so many railway carriages, they rejected.

Moreover, this rejection didn't simply come out of slaphappy youth without experience. It expressed the deliberate policy of those older and more-experienced members who had been elected L.S.O. directors. The L.S.O. does not pay its members regular salaries. It pays fees for the work actually done, in rehearsals, recordings, performances. Its members are very much on piecework jobs, and apart from promotion to front desks, the extent of their earnings depends on their own efforts. And they are not discouraged but encouraged to take outside work, and for the same reason that many of the younger members mentioned, to escape from dulling orchestral routine, to sharpen their musical wits, to enlarge and enrich their experience. But we must not forget that not all their members have complete faith in this policy. In this and in other matters, as I soon discovered, there can be some quite sharp disagreement among these men, but fortunately only when they are talking things over and not when they are playing their instruments together. Once on the platform they provide us with an example of collective talent and disciplined ability unmatched in any of the arts in Britain. Do I believe then that the L.S.O. offers us a higher level of performance than, say, the heavily subsidized National Theatre or the Royal Shakespeare Company? Certainly I do.

So, by determined hook or by lucky crook, we have here a great orchestra of which we have every reason to be proud. And it has arrived at a time—thanks to both air transport and recording—when the appreciation and the resulting influence of a great orchestra can be world-wide. Among London's exports, as well as among its pleasures, are the elegance and excitement, the delicacy and fire, of the L.S.O. And so far, so good. But those of us who have been going to concerts for the last fifty years are certain of one thing in musical history—that symphonic orchestras can come up and then they can go down. They can enchant us one year, and then several seasons later make us feel they oughtn't to be playing in public. Our memories are cluttered with the ruins of fine orchestras. To climb to the top is not easy; to stay there in all weathers is even more difficult. And knowing this, and liking as I do the musicians personally and enjoying immensely—and feeling

[146

deeply grateful for—the music they offer me, I cannot escape from a certain anxiety, a chilling touch of uneasiness. They may disagree in private, but on and on they go, out to Daytona, back from Daytona, ready for another month there next year, with a confidence that has a faint and not unpleasing hint of swagger in it, like the way they perform some works that are very much their own. I am completely and most devotedly on their side, but I cannot help wondering and then hoping rather hard. It is as if there were 100 men pledged to exhibit some flawless porcelain in the Royal Festival Hall, and when I catch sight of them all the 100 are carrying a vase 200 feet long across Waterloo Bridge. And either rain or darkness is falling and it is nearly the rush hour.

3

Who can take charge of a symphony orchestra and be completely responsible for it *musically*? Well, we know who can't, so it might be a good first move to clear them off the floor at once. Committees—academic, civic, H.M. Government—are out; so are groups, any size, balanced between culture and social prominence; so are rich men wanting to do some conducting; and so of course are authors who fancy they know a little about orchestral music and also imagine they possess a piercing insight into human nature. After allowing a few moments for the dust to settle, we now see there are three possibilities: a special type of conductor; a certain kind of impresario or general manager; a board of player-directors. A compromise solution might be provided by two of these, giving-and-taking at all hours; but any attempt to combine the three will move immediately towards uproar and chaos.

The special type of conductor is not simply one of those 'permanent' or 'principal' conductors that British orchestras are always announcing, with an air of triumph too often premature. Many of these permanents or principals keep flying in from Zurich or Geneva and are back at London Airport before the Festival Hall cleaners have swept the place after their concert of the night before. They don't, so to speak, live with the orchestra. They don't hire or fire anybody. They are not really *responsible* for the orchestra. For all they know—or perhaps care—the boys might be spending most of their time, between concerts, playing shove ha'penny. There could be a crisis in the orchestra, with perhaps half the woodwind walking out, and its so-called 'permanent conductor', who might be anywhere from Cologne to Los Angeles, wouldn't necessarily know anything about it. This couldn't happen with

[148

the special type of conductor. He is in charge and always on the spot.

If the orchestra needs some training, he is a trainer; if some coaching, he is a coach. If the orchestra has at last achieved the standard he requires, he maintains that standard even if by this time his men loathe him. (We are told that Mahler, a ruthless perfectionist, came to be hated by everybody employed in the Vienna Opera.) Most of these trainer-conductors have been martinets of the steely sort, respected and admired but not loved by their players, but in some rare instances a musician with an unusual temperament has contrived to be trainer-conductor-impresario without a complete loss of geniality, retaining the affection of his players. An obvious example of this very rare type is Beecham, who carefully picked his men, coached them in his own style, and then, in 1932, dazzled musical England with his new London Philharmonic as if he had just set fire to a rocket. And this orchestra, unlike others severely trained elsewhere, had not only discipline but also its own special verve, its suggestion of panache, like the L.S.O. today. The best recent example of a successful trainer-conductor is probably George Szell, who has forged, hammered, tempered the Cleveland Orchestra into a magnificent instrument. Its standard is very high indeed; but if like me, deplorably perhaps, you enjoy just a little extra edge, a touch of swashbuckle, you cannot help noticing, when you see close-ups of the Cleveland men on television, that they do watch their conductor rather anxiously, as if at no point will they gloriously let go and triumphantly pour it all out.

The L.S.O. we know today—and that really means at this moment of writing—is obviously in no need of any trainer, any coach. But just because its standard *is* so high, it could be argued that it should have one of these iron-willed conductors, no 'permanent' who keeps popping in and out but a man who never lets it long out of his sight, whose duty it is to make sure that on no occasion does the orchestra fall below that high

149]

standard, and to bully, cajole, inspire, when he thinks his men are feeling rather stale. (Here we must remember that the English—and I will throw in the Australians, as there are several of them in the L.S.O.—soon feel bored, chiefly because they are imaginative people pretending to be unimaginative. This is something very few of our politicians understand.) But conductors capable of this duty are very hard to find. And it is no use anybody asking why some young British conductor shouldn't be given a chance. This is not a young man's job. It demands long experience, age and weight. And here we cannot afford the salaries the richer American orchestras can offer. Moreover, a conductor of this sort will have to live here most of the year, which means he will be ferociously taxed. There are sound fiscal reasons why so many conductors are always popping in and out; in this way they are able to buy a hundred good cigars and a bottle or two of old brandy. So in the end it may be the Treasury that robs us of an orchestra maintaining the highest possible standard.

So much for the special type of conductor. The next possibility is a certain kind of impresario or general manager. And he is even harder to find than the conductor. He must know about music and understand symphonic orchestras; he must know what players ought to be hired or fired, and in his concern for a standard of performance he must be ruthless, apparently stony-hearted. (I couldn't tackle the job. Could you?) Given these qualifications, he enjoys one important advantage over the conductor or the board of player-directors. He does his listening not inside the performance but *outside* it, where the critics and the audiences are. He can therefore be more detached. Never mind how draughty the platform is, how many colds are there among the players, what sort of sound is coming from the orchestra? There may be a loss of cameraderie but there should be a gain in sharp criticism. After all, the conductor has to have an orchestra, the players have to have an orchestra, but an impresario may not want an orchestra

[150

at all unless it reaches the standard he has in mind. In this respect he is in the strongest position of the three.

I know no better example, in recent years, of what an impresario-manager of this kind can achieve than Walter Legge's creation of the Philharmonia, for some years the best symphony orchestra in Britain. Undoubtedly Legge's connection with E.M.I. and all its recording facilities and opportunities gave him enormous help, but even so his personal achievement was quite remarkable. He assembled comparatively quickly an orchestra of fine promise, kept on it a sharp eye and an even sharper ear, weeded out and improved this section and that, and arranged for it to be conducted by Klemperer and von Karajan, both formidable personalities but widely different in temperament and style. The Philharmonia troops would be steadily marching along under Klemperer one week, and then, a week or two later, would be blazing away under von Karajan: it was almost like a musical *blitzkrieg*. And if any would-be symphonic impresario should be reading this page—and he will have to be knowledgeable, untiring, tactful on Tuesday and ruthless on Wednesday—then I advise him to consult the astonishing Walter Legge, who also disproves Sacha Guitry's contention that all successful impresarios speak every language with a foreign accent, as if arriving from some completely unknown country.

We come now to the third possibility—a board of player-directors taking complete charge of the orchestra in what we might call musical self-government-de-luxe. There would have to be some sort of manager or general secretary, but he would be merely running the office. And I must add in all fairness that just before the Daytona visit and during it all the functions and responsibilities of a manager or general secretary were taken over by the player-directors, who seemed to me admirably competent. But this was a short-term affair, sensible men coping with a crisis; as a long-term policy, with the board taking on complete *musical* responsibility, replacing both the autocratic conductor and the masterful impresario, it may raise up some doubts. The musicians I talked to in Daytona Beach were not unanimous about this policy. (They were not unanimous about anything, which is one reason—the other being that my brain had turned to mush, as I declared much earlier—why I left Daytona feeling confused and uncertain.) For example, while some of them more than hinted that they had found Ernest Fleischmann too bossy and arbitrary, one or two others were ready to say that the present high standard of the L.S.O. owed much to him.

Then again, is it necessarily true, as Barry Tuckwell declared it was, that players are the best judges of their fellow players? It sounds reasonable, and on a short-term basis it probably is. But is it still reasonable if we take a longer term, extending over years and not months? Doesn't it assume too easily a generally-accepted critical high standard in the orchestra? Brown, Jones, Green and Robinson, still at their best, feel that their neighbour on the platform, Smith, ought to go because he is slipping. But if Brown, Jones, Green and Robinson are also slipping and are no more aware of it than Smith is, no judgment is possible; and the whole orchestra may be on the move towards mediocrity. Remember, under this system of complete self-government there is nobody with authority listening to it *on the outside.*

I don't see principals turning themselves into official listeners on the nights when they are not appearing with the L.S.O. Either they would be busy with other kinds of music or they would be taking a night off. Unless it has radically changed its policy since Daytona, the L.S.O. does not expect its principals to take their places at every performance. This is partly because the directors want the various sub-principals to gain experience in leading their sections. And one of the principals, an extremely conscientous and sensitive type, told me that while he didn't altogether condemn this policy, he was discovering already that he and his section were not as close

[152

as they had been, that there was some loss, slight but worrying, of understanding. He may have been showing himself to be unduly conscientious and sensitive. His fellow principals may not know any such anxiety and may be entirely content with this policy. Which brings us to another reason for it that is concerned with sub-principals gaining experience.

An orchestra with virtuosi-principals not under a long contract, not paid regular salaries, is living splendidly but dangerously. These are musicians who don't need an orchestra: they can accept engagements as soloists, they can spend more and more time with chamber music, they can take advanced classes. If they want to leave the orchestra, nobody can stop them. So they must be humoured. If they are feeling stale and bored, they can be left out of a few concerts. This can mean that while their names may be appearing on the programmes, heading their sections in the list of L.S.O. personnel, actually they may not be playing. In a recent notice of the L.S.O., highly praising its performance, there was a sardonic addition in parenthesis—*first eleven*. This told its readers in effect that all the principals were performing in this particular concert, unlike other occasions when some of them might be missing. This means, to put it brutally, that the L.S.O., which favours stiff prices, might take your money and not deliver the goods it has been offering. Not that I am accusing its directors of deliberately working a confidence trick. They are honest men, but they are trying to walk a tightrope. They have to work with a number of brilliant musicians who want to play in an orchestra and at the same time don't want to play in an orchestra.

This may be the chief reason why it is so difficult to keep a symphony orchestra on a high level. (Especially in a huge city like London, very different from Cleveland, Ohio.) A man content to play in one, month in and month out, year in and year out, may be steady and reliable—but dull. A man who is much better than this, anything but dull, may yawn at this prospect of month in, month out, year in, year out, blowing or

153]

fiddling away with ninety other fellows. Facing this difficulty, the L.S.O. directors—and indeed the members who elect them—have decided to live gloriously but dangerously, swaying on the tightrope, with arrows barbed with *first eleven* or *second eleven* whizzing past them.

Though much may happen before these pages are printed and bound, I am ready to admit that this complete self-government, for all its tightrope walking, has presented to the public the aspect of a dazzling success, no matter what desperate decisions may have had to be made in the board room. (Did the Daytona adventure come out of one of these or was it cheerful daftness responding to cheerful daftness?) But this success may possibly be short-term. Members of an orchestra in absolute control of its musical policy must sooner or later run into deep trouble. And there may be nobody to warn them. They can be rejecting too much, not only the idea of a securely established, guaranteed orchestra, but also the possibility of a rigorous and genuinely permanent conductor, or of an impresario or general manager who insists upon strict discipline. They could be cheating themselves without knowing it. For though these men may be—and I have already said they are—exceptionally hard-working and enthusiastic musicians, this doesn't mean they are free from the illusions and self-deceptions that entice most of us into a trap. For example, we may genuinely believe we need more discipline, but at the same time, being able to make a choice, we may unconsciously prefer the master who will not be too hard upon us. With a self-governing orchestra, this could mean an easy smiling conductor, just when a frowning martinet is needed, an impresario who would be all compliments and champagne, a general manager always polite to everybody but never really coming alive. In other words, at the very time when a hard choice ought to be made, it might not be made. And the whole glorious enterprise might be quietly starting to slither down-hill. It has happened before in music; it is always happening in one activity or another; as if something, not our weakness but always taking advantage of our weakness, wants it to happen. In his poem, *Mending Wall*, Robert Frost begins, muttering darkly: *Something there is that doesn't love a wall.* And I think there may be something, coming out of chaos and old night, that doesn't love a symphony orchestra trying to keep going, not without a touch of swagger, at its highest pitch. But let us end with Frost:

> Before I built a wall I'd ask to know
> What I was walling in or walling out,
> And to whom I was like to give offence.
> Something there is that doesn't love a wall,
> That wants it down. . . .

I spend so little time in London now, attend so few concerts there (though I make an effort for some L.S.O. occasions), that perhaps I ought to be sharply discouraged from writing a word about music in London. However, this begins as a confession. When I am abroad, as I often am, I find myself boasting—and I am rather given to boasting—about music in London, the extent and variety of it, four or five symphony orchestras all eager to play for us, to say nothing of visits from provincial or foreign orchestras—and so on and so forth and so on. I can hear myself hard at it, a bragging and boring old codger. What I say is true enough as far as it goes, but it does not go far enough to be the whole truth. The fact is that when I consider the London musical scene, perhaps after scanning the advertisements in Saturday morning's papers, I often catch myself feeling uneasy, vaguely dissatisfied. All these orchestras crying 'Listen, listen!', scrambling in and out of the Royal Festival Hall!

We will halt there a moment or two, though I am still confessing. I don't *really* like our R.F.H., as it is called in orchestra work sheets. I think I would pay double to be back in the old Queen's Hall. I know, I know, it wasn't big enough to satisfy our post-war economics. And it could be very stuffy

155]

in the circle, where I usually sat and where, after a long day, perhaps rehearsing or rewriting a new play, I have half-slept through almost every slow movement in the classical repertoire. But it could blend and colour and warm orchestral sound in a magical way, far beyond the R.F.H. can even attempt to do. (And don't tell me the magic was in me then, not in the sound, because I know better.) And with the old Queen's Hall, you could stroll up, just slip through a door, and then be with the music. On some nights at the R.F.H. the sight of the river is rewarding, but the place seems to make such a portentous fuss about your attending a concert there, as if it were a Coronation or some other gigantic helping of flummery. It is as if the Hall and all the fusspot arrangements leading into it had really been built for senior politicians, Privy Councillors, Lord Mayors, High Sheriffs and the like, not for musicians and lovers of music. Schubert would not have been allowed in the place. It makes you feel you ought to be doing something more important in there than listening to music, something to do with national security or productivity or surcharges on surtax. It cries out for large-scale resolutions and amendments and votes of thanks, not *allegrettos* and *adagios*. If music in London is turning into big business, then the R.F.H. is its home—all those boxes looking like half-opened tills. Yes, yes, the waterside can be charming, the river front and the entrance hall and the stairs are imposing, the seating arrangements are excellent, the lighting is efficient, and the acoustics are as good as modern expertise can make them—but Oh my Portland Place and Queen's Hall long ago, long ago!

All that was in parenthesis, and possibly a piece of self-indulgence, but it wasn't entirely digressive. The fact that the orchestras seemed to be hurrying to get into the Royal Festival Hall may be partly responsible for my feeling of unease, vague dissatisfaction: they all want to go where I don't want to go. There is also a suggestion—though I am not pretending this is fair comment—of a musical rat race.

[156

When I was a boy in the North, all the chapels of any size wanted to do the *Messiah* as a Christmas piece. But they were all so eager to get in first that performances of the *Messiah* came earlier and earlier, so that weeks before Christmas people had had enough of it. What has this to do with symphonic music in London? Nothing in actual fact, but when I read the Saturday morning advertisements, or indeed the seasonal brochures sent out by orchestras, I seem to get a whiff of the same atmosphere: let's jump in with that Beethoven, that Tschaikowsky, that new man playing the Rachmaninoff No. 2. We are being offered a lot of music—and it isn't bad and not badly performed —but still the whole musical scene, not observed from the inside but from the outside, makes me feel uncomfortable. It appears to be too highly charged with competitiveness.

This is, if you like, a personal prejudice. I don't know and don't care if competition is good and healthy for breakfast foods, patent medicines, toilet preparations, but I have always felt it is bad and unhealthy for the arts. It takes them into the wrong atmosphere. I pass for a fairly aggressive type, not an ultra-sensitive writer, shrinking and wincing in his ivory tower, but it is a fact that never, never, never, have I felt myself to be competing against some other novelists or dramatists. Whatever publishers, theatre managers, critics or the public may think and feel, I don't live in that kind of world. It exists for sales managers, not artists and the arts. So this over-competitive aspect of the crowded scene of London's music repels me. I want something different.

When I say that, I don't mean that I feel some orchestras should be hurried out of the scene, to be tried and executed. That isn't my concern here, and if it were I doubt if I would be competent to deal with it. What I do mean is that I should like to see one great orchestra taken right out of the competition, the race, the scramble. It would be above the present battle. It would follow serenely its own policy, without reference to any others. It would be so situated that it could afford to ignore quantity and concentrate upon quality. It would not be for ever running about, playing its head off. It would not be employing razors to cut firewood. Like many important orchestras elsewhere, it would repeat its programmes, thus allowing itself more time for rehearsal, and, in London, giving its public the chance to attend one or other of these identical concerts. And one of them would, I hope, always be recorded for television and radio. In addition, suitable items would go, as soon as possible, on to records. And here, defying the record companies and their sound engineers, I want to suggest that some of these records need not be of special studio performances but could be taken direct from concerts. I know the arguments against recording live performances— some defects that the conductors feel they can remove, the inferior quality of sound, the audience noises—but now and again, as certain records prove, a sense of immediacy and the actual excitement of the concert performance are somehow communicated. Finally, if we add the rewards of all these activities to a handsome subsidy, which a great orchestra of this sort could justly claim, we should no longer have a permanent conductor, an impresario or manager, or a board of directors, wondering how and where another few thousand pounds can be earned. That wolf will have been banished from the door.

This mention of the hovering wolf reminds me of a point I have been wishing to make all along. The Barbican scheme giving the L.S.O. a hall of its own could perhaps establish it —or do much to establish it—as London's great permanent orchestra. And of course I had the L.S.O. in mind throughout the last paragraph. Even as it is today, not yet free from anxiety, still having to run around and push and compete, the L.S.O. is a remarkable orchestra, with enormous prestige both at home and abroad. But now, so that I can make my point, we must leave this grandeur and consider the poor old Hallé. It is, of course, still worth listening to—especially under

Barbirolli—but for years and years now it has been under-manned and overworked and almost battling for its life. So why drag it in here? Because the imperiously magnificent L.S.O. of today would have been considerably less magnificent if the Hallé had not supplied it with so many splendid musicians. I have not worked this out—I am too lazy—but I soon discovered in Daytona that the ranks of the L.S.O., front desks as well as back desks, are thick with men who once played in Manchester. So far as the present L.S.O. has had one nursery, it has been in the North. And, to my mind, that is how things should be, no matter what grand Barbican plans might be adopted. Let the nursery be fed and warmed and enlarged and the Hallé no longer under-manned and overworked, its battle won at last.

Would this great orchestra I have in mind, this Barbican-based and out-of-the-R.F.H.-scramble L.S.O., be allowed to attach itself, for a whole month, to an annual summer festival, not only playing as an orchestra but also doing chamber music, taking classes, teaching students, in fact turning some place into an important musical centre? It would indeed, if I had any say in the matter. (And I shan't have, so not to worry!) Daytona Beach then—and sun and sand and shrimp boils and yacht races and parties and brown contented wives and kids happily roistering? I am afraid not, but remember I am grandly —though perhaps a trifle idly—planning now, not facing immediate reality. If I jerk my attention from things-as-they-ought-to-be to things-as-they-are, then I have to admit that a month in Daytona, though not the best setting for our finest orchestra, remains a workable idea as well as a huge daft lark. But Daytona would not figure in *my* plans for *my* orchestra for one good simple reason. It is in Florida, not in England.

I want to see an English town turned into a musical centre every summer, with either orchestral concerts or chamber music each night, with an Institute and master classes and a Student Orchestra and the rest. (And I would add fairly

159]

informal tea-time talks on composers or particular works.) I remember with affection and some regret the old Malvern Drama Festival of the 1930s, where you could be certain of a week's excellent play-going, with every night a different play, ranging from *Gammer Gurton's Needle* to the latest Shaw, and you had a pleasant small town and some capital walking country, and the whole thing was on a manageable friendly scale. This scale would have to be enlarged, of course, for a musical festival. There would have to be a concert hall of reasonable dimensions. (And we are short of them.) Far more accommodation would be necessary. But even so, cities must be avoided. No man in his senses wants to spend even a week of his summer in Birmingham, Manchester or Leeds. It is possible that the sort of town I have in mind, a place that can look as if it is enjoying a festival and yet has a large concert hall, simply does not exist in this country. And if it doesn't, then I would never dream of blaming the L.S.O. for returning to Daytona every year. The good work must go on somewhere. The trumpets that are silenced here must fly again over the sea.